Mum is the gr...
cook ever even better
than Jamie Oliver I'm
Sure that everybody
will Like her cooking
She makes the best toud
in the hole ever so
everybody would say she
is the best cook around

from
Charlie Bilton

When I'm older I want
to work for mum so I can
Serve her gorgeos food

Disclaimer: many dogs were spoilt with gravy bones during the making of this book.

This book was made by cookbook writing novices, therefore even though there have been countless re-reads there may still be a few grammatical mistakes.

To Kirsten,

Happy Cooking
With Love
Ali xx

This book is dedicated to my Mum (Granny Holtby, Auntie Sheila, GG, Alice), may she still be dishing up deliciousness.

Introduction:

My love of cooking and food is completely attributed to my mother, Sheila, or Alice, as my father Keith called her, who was a self-taught cook. She trained as a secretary in Eastbourne and had never really cooked at all when she met and fell in love with my father. Keith was a first-generation East Yorkshire farmer and when they married and moved into their first house in Foston-on-the-Wolds meals were really on a trial and error basis only. Luckily, there was always my Uncle Snuff (who would eat anything) to tackle the remainders - but even he said some things laid heavily on his stomach!

Over the years, my mother became a really accomplished cook. She prepared three cooked meals a day for her growing family, until she decided to open a shop with her sister Shirley in Bridlington. Suddenly, Keith now had to cope with only two cooked meals a day. Fortunately for my father and his three young daughters, this was only a temporary measure, as Mum gave up her share in the shop and came back home when I told her about the delicious tomato ketchup sandwich I had eaten for my tea at a neighbour's house! Needless to say, normal service was soon resumed and thereafter wholesome, hot food was again on the table three times a day.

When my mother was entertaining, she went all out. She and her friends loved to cook for each other - and they loved to pass around recipes amongst themselves. There are many that my sisters and I still cook now, such as Mrs Twiddle's Delight, Granny Farnie's Chutney, Ada's Superior Piccalilli, Continental Gateau and Norwegian Cream. They don't feature in this book but I will definitely keep these and the other recipes for posterity...and possibly, another book.

Because we lived on a farm, our meals at home consisted of home-grown vegetables, home-reared meat and fish caught by my father in Foston Beck. Always nourishing and delicious. Many foods still evoke our family meals at Church Farm and nothing tasted as sweet as the peaches that Dad grew in the greenhouse, lovingly tended every year. Peas from the pod, strawberries from the plant, the first Arran Pilot new potatoes of the year, boiled with baby carrots, always dripping with melted butter and freshly chopped chives, asparagus, butter and salt - simple but delicious. If only we realised then how lucky we were to be eating fresh food with no food miles; and only seasonal produce, just the ethos that we are trying to return to now.

Luckily for me, I had the most fantastic cookery teacher at school, Mrs Brown. She was modern, encouraging and full of fun, so my food career began. After studying at Oxford Poly and Leith's of London, I worked in the city with Rebecca Staight, where we cooked for Directors Dining Rooms (now a thing of the past) and for Richard Rogers Architects. I travelled all over London in a Ford Fiesta, delivering and cooking food.

Then I followed my boyfriend, Howard, to Spain and started my own catering business. Luckily, I met Jill Simpson and Simpson & Holtby was born. We hit Gibraltar in the boom years of the financial industry when many banks, insurance brokers and trust fund companies opened. Simpson & Holtby catered for most of the opening parties. We had a great time both at work and play. Here again we cooked from seasonal local produce going to the market every day in La Linea to buy freshly caught fish, whilst under the watchful gaze of the local police ,who sat drinking large brandies with their morning coffee. Whilst I lived in Spain I cooked for the legendary Marlboro Honda Formula 1 racing team. when Ayrton Senna and Alain Prost drove for them. We cooked for the team and visiting VIP's, 3 of us catering for up to 80 people from the kitchen of a motorhome. A very good exercise in learning how to be space efficient.

Then when married and with a young son, Tom, we moved to Hong Kong and my culinary world opened even further. My knowledge of Thai food was very limited but here it was in abundance. Bangkok was only a two-hour flight away, there was such an amazing array of colours and flavours, fruit as I'd never tasted it before, street food was a must. And a visit to the Hawker market in Singapore is absolute culinary heaven.

Then back to the UK with two small boys, back to my Mum's kitchen and my UK food journey continued. I brought back with me dishes from all over the world and at first, frustration, at not being able to source the ingredients. Slowly but surely, with the increase in cookery programmes and the ease of travel, exotic ingredients began to appear on supermarket shelves and I could once again indulge in my love for Thai food and introduce it to others. There are quite a few Thai style dishes included in this collection.

More recently, my partner, Robert and I have been lucky enough to travel extensively in Italy, either sailing the beautiful coastline or driving the tiniest of roads in our old Volvo; mostly spending time in Sardinia, learning how to make pasta from the best teachers, Italian grandmothers. Each Nonna has their own technique - but of course, each one is the right one!

So now it's my turn to pass on my favourite recipes, some of which have sentimental value and some of which have been already passed on to others, either during my time at the Yorkshire Wolds Cookery School, or in my previous lives cooking in far-flung places.

All these recipes are ones that I love and I hope you enjoy them as much as I and others do and have done, in the past. I hope they carry on travelling.

Happy cooking!

Charlie, Tom and I at Charlie's 21st 2015

Spanish Grand Prix team 1988 (I'm 2nd left from Ayrton Senna)

Dad and pelican in Sitia, Crete

Uncle Snuff

Mum, Polly Barley and Dot Hopper, Bridlington Beach circa. 1955

Press Association Opening in Howden with Prince Charles, 2005

contents:

contents:

breakfast and snacks

Sometimes breakfast has to be swift and ready to go, here are a few ideas for that rushed morning to keep you going! Alphonso mangoes in season from June through to September, well worth seeking out from your nearest oriental supermarket.

bircher muesli

ingredients:

200g rolled oats
375ml apple juice
25g pumpkin seeds
25g sunflower seeds
2 apples
125g plain yoghurt
a selection of berries of your choice

method:

-put the rolled oats in a bowl with the apple juice and leave to soak, covered, for an hour, or overnight in the fridge.
-heat a small frying pan to a medium heat and toast the seeds until they start to pop and become golden brown. Store in a jam jar until required.
-when ready to eat the bircher, core, but do not peel the apples, then coarsely grate into the oats.
-add the yoghurt and mix well.
-serve with the berries and toasted seeds on top.
-this will keep for a couple of days in the fridge and is perfect for that breakfast on the go.

energy balls

ingredients:

120g hazelnuts (see. p. 131 for tips)
200g pitted medjool dates
2 tbsp raw cocoa powder
2 tbsp rolled oats

method:

-preheat the oven to 180°C/350°F/Gas4.
-toast the hazelnuts for about 10 minutes until golden brown, allow to cool.
-place the dates, nuts and cocoa powder in a food processor and blitz until the mixture starts to come together, if it is a bit dry add a drop or two of water.
-add the oats and pulse to bring together.
-using damp hands form into walnut sized balls, depending on the size you make it should do 10-12 balls.
-store in an airtight container for up to 5 days in the fridge, or 2 months in the freezer.
-for variations add cocoa nibs, change the nuts for almonds, peanuts or cashews, add dried cranberries, sour cherries, raisins, roll in cocoa powder or hemp seeds- the variations are endless.

makes 10-12

mango lassi

ingredients:

1 very ripe mango, preferably Alphonso
100ml natural or low-fat yoghurt
a squeeze of lime juice
large pinch ground cardamom
½ tsp soft light brown sugar

method:

-peel and destone the mango. Dice the flesh and place in a small measuring jug.
-whizz with a stick blender until smooth.
-add the remaining ingredients and whizz together
-serve immediately.

serves 2

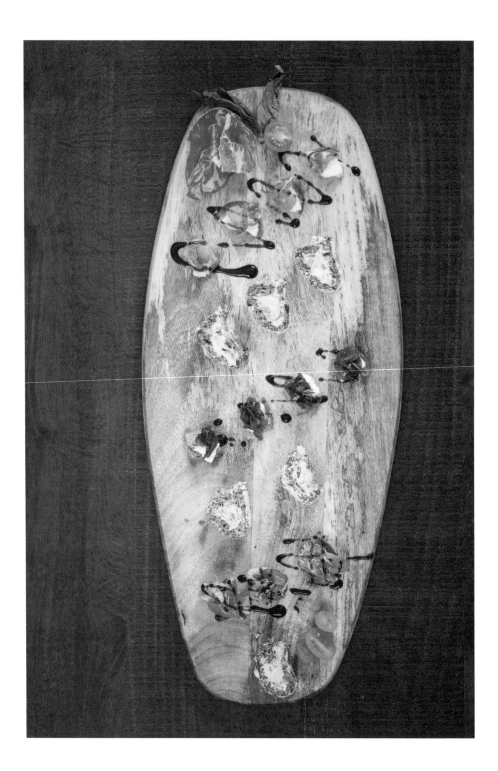

canapés

bruschetta with various toppings

ingredients:

French/Italian bread as small in diameter as you
can find
olive oil
salt and pepper

method:

-set the oven to 180°C/350°F/Gas3.
-cut the bread into 5mm slices and then cut into bitesize
pieces.
-put onto a roasting tray having dipped the bread into
olive oil on both sides.
-bake for 10-15 mins until brown, turning the bread over
after about 7 minutes. Keep an eye on them as they
overcook very quickly.
-store in an airtight container for 2 weeks.

toppings:

anything you like really but the following work well;

-goat's cheese and caramelised onion, see recipe for filo parcels (p. 19)

-pear, Parma ham, and Yorkshire Blue drizzled with balsamic glaze

-crab meat, smoked salmon and brown shrimp

-prawns with cream and dill

-beef fillet, Yorkshire Blue and horseradish

-tomato, basil and mozzarella, drizzled with balsamic glaze

Bruschetta are a great standby for a quick canapé to put together when you have friends round, or if you just fancy a bite before dinner. They keep in a sealed container for up to 2 weeks. I love messing about with toppings for these and coming up with different combinations. Here are six suggestions but let your imagination go crazy, they also make great croutons.

The images show how to fold the parcels, once you get the hang of it you can whip up a big batch in no time, which can be kept in the freezer and cooked from frozen in an emergency canape situation!

filo parcels with goat's cheese and caramelised onion

ingredients:

method:

for the caramelised onion:
450g red onions, thinly sliced
2 tbsp rapeseed oil
2 tbsp demerera sugar
2 large sprigs of rosemary
1 tbsp crème de cassis
1 tbsp balsamic vinegar

for the parcels:
80g butter
10 sheets filo pastry (if possible Theo's, available in Tesco)
125g goat's cheese log/soft goat's cheese
caramelised onion
salt and pepper

-first make the caramelised onion, put the sliced onions, oil, sugar and rosemary into a large sauté pan over a medium heat, cover and sweat for 20 minutes.
-check to see if the onions are soft, if so add the remaining ingredients (if not cook until soft), turn up the heat to high, cook until all liquid has disappeared, taking care not to burn. Allow the onion to cool slightly.
-preheat the oven to 200°C/400°F/Gas6.
-cut the goat's cheese into 1 cm cubes.
-melt the butter in a pan.
-lay one sheet of filo pastry on a board with the shortest part facing you. Brush half way up with butter, fold the unbuttered half down over the buttered half to create 2 layers.

-brush the pastry again with butter and then cut into 5 vertical strips.
-place a piece of goat's cheese in the corner of each pastry strip top with caramelised onion. Season with salt and pepper.
-now fold the pastry over the cheese and onion to form a triangle, keep folding the triangle upwards until you have used up all the pastry.
-place the parcels on a baking sheet lined with baking parchment and brush with more melted butter.
-place in the preheated oven for 10-15 minutes until golden brown.

makes 50

variations:

1 pack mozzarella cut into small pieces (will be more than enough)
a handful of basil shredded
red pesto
-add salt and pepper at the end

feta cheese and oregano
-feta cheese chopped into cubes and sprinkled with dried oregano, salt and pepper

You will have more caramelised onions than you need, but this can be stored in a container for up to 2 weeks and used as a simple addition to a cheese board, quiche filling or a filling for a toasted cheese sandwich.

If you would like to freeze these parcels they can be layered between two sheets of baking parchment but don't brush with butter until you are ready to cook. Then place in the preheated oven for 10-15 minutes until golden brown, adding a couple of minutes more if cooking from frozen.

As a Yorkshire born and bred girl I couldn't write a book without including these. The Yorkshire pudding batter is the same for the large sized ones too. They take longer to cook, 20 mins at 220°C and then turn down the oven to 180°C without opening the door and cook for a further 10 minutes. Approximately 5 eggs makes 12 deep muffin tin sized yorshire puddings. Both types of puddings keep well in the freezer. Let them cool down and open freeze on a tray before bagging up and freezing in a ziplock bag. Reheat from frozen at 180°C for 10 minutes. The sage, apple, onion and pork are a little more effort, but these are especially for Harry Atkin, his favourite, if you prepare the apple and onion in wedges it works well as an alternative to apple sauce with Alison Sutcliffe's amazing pork loin, the best I have ever had the pleasure to cook and eat.

mini yorkshire puddings

ingredients:

2 eggs, measure their liquid weight
same weight of eggs in plain flour
half the weight of the eggs in milk
half the weight of the eggs in water
pinch of salt
beef dripping or rapeseed oil

method:

-weigh the eggs into a jug, add the flour, milk, water and salt.
-mix until smooth with a hand blender, or better still in a blender if you have one.
-leave to stand for 2 hours, or overnight if possible.

-preheat the oven to 220°C/425°F/Gas7, and place a knob of beef dripping or a little rapeseed oil in each hole of 2x24 cup mini muffin tins, or 4x12 cup mini muffin tins (if you only have 1 tin you can cook these in smaller batches). when the oven is hot put the tins in to heat up the fat for 5 minutes.
-take the batter out of the fridge, stir, and add 1 tbsp cold water, stir that in.
-remove the tins from the oven carefully as they will be very hot and smoky. Pour the batter into the moulds, half way up.
-put the tins back in the oven and bake for 10-12 minutes until the puddings are risen and golden brown.
-the puddings can be made ahead of time, allowed to cool or be frozen. then reheated at 180°C for 5 minutes from cold or 7 minutes from frozen.

makes 48

variations:

roast beef and horseradish: 1 trimmed beef fillet tail, horseradish sauce. Rub the fillet tail with rapeseed oil and fry until golden brown in a very hot frying pan, place in a preheated oven at 180°C for 10 minutes, allow to cool and then cut into small pieces. place a dab of horseradish sauce on each hot Yorkshire pudding, followed by a piece of beef.

sausage and mustard creme fraiche: 8 chipolata sausages, 2 tbsp crème fraîche mixed with 1 tsp whole grain mustard, 1 tsp dijon mustard. Cook the sausages at 180°C for 15 minutes, cut each sausage into 6, spoon a little of the mustardy crème fraîche on to each hot Yorkshire pud, and top with a piece of sausage.

pork, sage, apple and onion: 350g pork tenderloin, 50ml dry cider, ½ small red onion, peeled and roughly chopped, 1 cox apple, peeled and cut into small pieces, 15g butter, 1 tbsp demerara sugar, 5g sage leaves, plus a few for dressing, 1 tbsp brandy. Brown the pork tenderloin in a frying pan, add the cider and then place in an oven preheated to 180°C for 15 minutes. Allow to cool and cut into bite size mini yorkshire pudding filling-sized pieces, keep in the cooking juices. To make the filling: melt half of the butter in a large frying pan, add ½ tbsp demerara sugar melt over a medium to high heat and add the red onion. Cook until softened and caramelised, stirring every now and again. Remove from the pan, then add the remaining butter and sugar and cook the apple pieces in the same way. Put the onions back in with the apples and add the chopped sage. Turn up the heat and add the brandy, cook stirring for a couple of minutes. Keep warm if using straight away, or gently reheat before placing a little in each pudding. Warm the pork through in a saucepan gently and place a piece of pork on top and dress with a small piece of sage.

salmon and wasabi rolls on cucumber

ingredients:

150g full fat cream cheese at room temperature
½-1tsp wasabi paste
10g fresh dill, chopped
freshly ground black pepper
200g thinly sliced smoked salmon
1 cucumber

method:

-place the cream cheese, wasabi and dill in a bowl and mix well. season to taste with black pepper.
-to make the rolls, lay the smoked salmon onto a sheet of clingfilm on a chopping board and form a rectangle of 30 x 10 cm.
-spread some of the cream cheese mixture evenly over the top about 5mm thick.
-roll the smoked salmon lengthways as tightly as possible using the clingfilm. Place in the fridge to firm up. Repeat with the remaining smoked salmon. At this point the rolls can be kept in the fridge for 2 days or frozen well wrapped for up to 2 months.
-cut the cucumber into 5mm rounds and cut with a 4cm cutter to form perfect rounds.
-remove the salmon from the fridge and slice into 1 ½ cm rounds and place on the top of the cucumber.
-garnish with a sprig of dill and serve.

makes 30

Delicious bites of smoked salmon greatness, just given a bit of a kick with wasabi. I use the fabulous Staal Smokehouse salmon, and if you ask Justin may be able to cut it in long slices for you.

I have been making this since I can remember, I first made it whilst working for the great Rebecca Staight in London where I cooked in Directors' Dining Rooms in the city. I have adapted the recipe and it always proves a winner. It freezes well and is always a good standby to have. You can change the filling for cream cheese with a squeeze of lemon juice and dill, and slices of smoked salmon, or add some hot smoked salmon to the cream cheese.

spinach roulade

see p. 131 for tips and tricks

ingredients:

method:

for the roulade:
1 x 200g bag of washed, ready to eat baby leaf spinach
200ml milk
¼ of a nutmeg, grated
25g butter
25g plain flour
3 eggs, separated

for the filling:
150ml crème fraîche
1 tbsp of red pesto
6 sun blushed or sun dried tomatoes in oil, sliced
large handful of fresh basil leaves, shredded
4 spring onions, trimmed and finely chopped
50g grated parmesan
salt and pepper to taste

-preheat the oven at 180°C/375°F/Gas4
-pierce the bag of spinach and put into a microwave on full power for two minutes. (if you don't have a microwave put the spinach into a pan with a splash of cold water, cover with a lid and cook on full heat shaking the pan occassionally until the spinach is wilted). Put the spinach into a colander to drain, taking care not to scald yourself with the steam.
-warm the milk and nutmeg just to boiling point in a saucepan.
-melt the butter and add the flour, let it cook over low heat to form a 'blonde' roux. When the roux is cooked through, whisk in the nutmeg infused milk.
-turn the heat up and whisk the sauce until it is a very thick consistency. Take off heat and leave to cool.
-transfer the cooled sauce into a food processor. Squeeze as much moisture out of the cooked spinach as possible and add to the white sauce. Season with salt and pepper.

-blend for a minute or two until the spinach and sauce are thoroughly mixed. Add the egg yolks and whizz again, transfer the spinach mixture to a mixing bowl.
-in a separate bowl whisk the egg whites to form stiff peaks. You should be able to turn the bowl upside down and the whisked eggs stay put!
-fold the whisked egg whites gently into the spinach mix a little at a time.
-line 2 swiss roll tins with baking parchment (see p. 131 for tips and tricks) and divide the mixture between the two tins, spead out evenly, it should be very thin.
-place into the preheated oven for 10-15 minutes.
-remove from the oven. Cover with damp greaseproof paper and a clean damp tea towel. Allow to cool.
-to make the filling, mix together the crème fraîche, pesto, sun blushed tomatoes, spring onions, basil and salt and pepper and mix thoroughly.
-to assemble: spread greaseproof paper onto the work surface and sprinkle with grated parmesan.
-turn the spinach roulade onto the parmesan covered paper.
-spoon the fillling misture onto the roulade and spread evenly right to the edges.
-lift a long edge of the greaseproof paper and fold the roulade gently to form a roll, half way to the centre.
-lift the opposite long edge of greaseproof paper (see picture) and gently fold again, forming a roll of the roulade to meet in the middle.
-wrap the roulade in the greaseproof paper and chill for at least an hour, or freeze for up to two months.
-to serve, unwrap the roulade and cut down lengthways along the centre.
-cut across to make about 32 portions.

starters and salads

beetroot cured salmon with celeriac slaw

ingredients:

500g salmon or sea trout, with the skin on cut into 2 pieces

for the cure:
15g fresh dill
30g rough sea salt crystals
25g caster sugar
3g black peppercorns
1 tbsp Raisthorpe orange, or other orange liqueur
½ lemon, zested and finely chopped
1 tsp finely chopped orange zest
100g raw beetroot

for the slaw:
75ml crème fraiche
1 gherkin
¼ tsp capers
½ tsp wholegrain mustard
¼ lemon, zested and chopped
½ tsp finely chopped orange zest
1 tbsp orange juice
pinch caster sugar
2 sprigs dill, finely chopped, stalks and all
100g celeriac

method:

-roughly chop the dill, including the stalks, and mix thoroughly in a bowl with salt and sugar.
-crush the peppercorns in a pestle and mortar and add to the salt cure. Add the orange liqueur, the lemon and orange zest.
-peel and coarsely grate the beetroot. Add to the cure mix.
-take a large sheet of tin foil and place a $1/3$ of the beetroot cure in the centre, lay one of the salmon fillets on top (skin side down), another $1/3$ of the cure then final salmon fillet (skin side up) and finally the remaining cure).
-wrap the salmon up securely in the foil parcel and then place in a ziplock bag. Place in a dish and then put a plate on the top, weigh it down with a heavy object. Leave to marinate in the fridge for 2-4 days. Turn the salmon daily.
-take out of the fridge, remove from the wrapping and pour away any juices. Scrape off the excess beetroot, rinse with cold water.
-slice the salmon very thinly from the flesh down to the skin. Set to one side whilst you make the salad.
-put the crème fraiche in a bowl, chop the gherkins, add to the cream along with capers, mustard, lemon and orange juice, zests and sugar. Season with salt and add the chopped dill.
-lastly peel and coarsely grate the celeriac (it will discolour very quickly), add to the creamy dressing. Leave for an hour and serve with the sliced fish, and some rye or multi-grain bread.

serves 4 as a starter, with plenty of salmon left over.

This is a stunning starter to prepare and amaze your guests with. You can also give the cured salmon as a gift for a foodie friend.

The salmon can be made in larger batches and frozen either as a whole or carved and kept for up to a month in the freezer.

twice baked salmon soufflé

ingredients:

200ml full cream milk
nutmeg
20g unsalted butter, plus extra for buttering
20g self raising flour
2 large eggs, separated
100g smoked salmon, finely chopped
2 tbsps fresh dill, finely chopped, stalks and all
4 tbsp double cream
about 2 tsp parmesan, grated
freshly ground black pepper

for the sauce:
200ml medium sweet white wine (Riesling or Hock is
particularly good)
5g fresh dill, finely chopped, stalks and all
200ml double cream
salt and freshly ground black pepper

4 dariole moulds or small ramekin dishes
4 small gratin dishes
1 deep roasting tin

method:

-preheat the oven to 190°C/375°F/Gas5.
-for the soufflé, put a good grind of nutmeg and the milk
into a saucepan and bring to just simmering point over a
medium heat. Remove from the heat and leave to infuse
for 15 minutes.
-melt the butter in a saucepan over a medium heat, whisk
in the flour to make a roux. Cook for 1 minute. Pour over
the milk and whisk continuously until it comes to the boil.
as soon as it thickens reduce the heat and simmer for 3
minutes, whisking occasionally.
-take off the heat and leave to cool for 20 minutes. Melt
a little butter and generously butter 4 (200ml) dariole
moulds or ramekins.
-beat the egg yolks into the cooled sauce
followed by the chopped dill. Stir in the salmon and
season generously with pepper.
-in a clean bowl, whisk the egg whites into soft peaks
with an electric whisk until they just hold their shape.
-fold in the egg whites carefully, a little at a time,
keeping as much air in the mixture as possible.
-spoon the mixture into the four well buttered dariole
moulds.

-place the moulds into a deep baking tin and pour boiling water around them so it comes to half way up the sides
of the moulds (if you use cold water it won't work, it must be boiling).
-put the tin on the middle shelf of the oven and cook for 25 minutes or until well risen and golden brown.
-remove the tin from the oven and then carefully lift out the dariole moulds onto a cooling rack. Allow to cool. The
soufflés will collapse completely.
-the soufflés can be refrigerated for up to 36 hours, still in the moulds, wrapped in cling film.
-for the sauce, pour the wine into a small saucepan, add the dill and bring to the boil uncovered, bubble furiously
until the wine has almost disappeared, then pour in the cream. Bring to the boil again and simmer for 2 minutes,
season to taste. This sauce can also be made in advance, kept in the fridge, and reheated when needed.
-when ready to serve, pre heat the oven to 220°C/425°F/Gas7. Take the soufflés out of the fridge and allow
them to reach room temperature. Turn out each soufflé by running a knife carefully around the edge to realease
the soufflé. If any soufflé sticks to the mould, scrape it out and rebuild, they will be fine. Place each soufflé upside
down onto four small buttered ovenproof dishes. Top with a tablespoon of double cream and a sprinkling of
parmesan.
-place the soufflés on the middle shelf of the oven and cook about 12 minutes until risen and golden.
-whilst the soufflés are in the oven reheat the sauce and as soon as the soufflés come out of the oven pour a little
sauce over each and serve immediately.

serves 4.

Such a great starter, easy to prepare and can be made three days in advance. It always impresses that
you can whip up a soufflé without any stress whatsoever!

31

scallops wrapped in pancetta with cream and dill sauce

ingredients:

4 large scallops
4-6 slices pancetta
4 small bamboo skewers

for the sauce:
60ml medium sweet white wine (Riesling is particularly good)
1 tbsp fresh dill, finely chopped, stalks and all
45ml double cream
salt and freshly ground black pepper

method:

-discard the white muscle from each scallop, and cut into 2 or 3 pieces depending on the size of the scallop. Wrap each in a slice of pancetta. Skewer onto a bamboo stick, 3 pancetta wrapped scallops per skewer.
-for the sauce, pour the wine into a small shallow pan and add the dill. Bring to a fast boil and reduce until there is only about 1 tbsp of liquid left. Add the cream and simmer for about 2 minutes. Season to taste. Keep warm.
-heat a small frying pan unitl hot and add the scallop skewers. Fry briskly for 1-2 minutes on each side until brown.
-remove the scallops from the skewers and place three on to a warmed plate. Surround with the cream and dill sauce. serve immediately.

serves 4 as a starter.

Using the same sauce as the soufflé (p. 31) this is a great little dish that cooks the scallops easily on skewers. It can also be eaten as a canapé on a chinese rice spoon with a little of the sauce underneath. The scallops can be prepared ahead, and frozen for up to a month, as long as the scallops were not previously frozen. The sauce can be made in advance, kept chilled or frozen for up to a month and reheated without danger of splitting.

thai beef salad

ingredients:

250g sirloin steak
15g fresh coriander on the stalk
15g fresh mint on the stalk
1-2 red chillies, finely chopped or 1 birdseye chilli,
finely chopped
1 clove of garlic, peeled and chopped
2.5 cm piece root ginger, peeled and chopped
2 stems lemongrass, tough outer layers removed and
finely slice the soft centre of the lemongrass (see p.
131)
1 tbsp fish sauce
3 tbsp lime juice
2 tsp palm sugar or soft, light brown sugar
4 kaffir lime leaves, stalks removed, rolled into a cigar
shape, very finely shredded
zest of 1 lime
60g red or black grapes, halved and
deseeded if necessary

to garnish:
reserved coriander and mint, chopped
50g cherry tomatoes, halved
¼ cucumber, cut into small pieces
a handful of salad leaves

method:

-first you need to cook the beef in advance.
-heat a griddle pan until smoking, sear the beef quickly
for 2 minutes each side.
-be careful not to overcook: it needs to be quite pink as
the lime juice in the dressing cooks the beef a bit further.
-allow to rest for 10 minutes.
-remove the coriander and mint from the stalks. Reserve
and chop finely 6 coriander stalks and 1 mint stalk, keep
the leaves for dressing the salad.
-pound together the chillies, garlic, chopped coriander
stalks, chopped mint stalk, ginger and lemongrass in a
pestle and mortar until you achieve a good paste.
-add the fish sauce, lime juice and palm sugar and blend
everything together.
-trim the steak of fat and any gristle and cut into thin
strips.
-when ready to serve, pile the grilled beef strips onto a
serving plate, pour the dressing over and sprinkle on the
lime leaves, lime zest and grapes.
-garnish with the reserved coriander and mint leaves,
tomatoes, cucumber and salad leaves.

serves 2 as a main course, or 4 as a starter.

I first tasted this dish when I was living in Hong Kong at a restaurant called The Chilli Club. We were warned that diners always entered through the door and left through the roof, they were not joking! I have adapted this to more western taste, but if you want to ramp it up, go ahead!

beetroot, crispy kale and red onion salad

ingredients:

700g cooked beetroot (see note), peeled and cut into
wedges
2 tbsp rapeseed oil
2 red onions, peeled, halved and cut into small wedges
1 tsp of dried oregano
2 tbsp balsalmic vinegar
salt and pepper
100g kale
1 tbsp rapeseed oil
30g rocket

method:

-preheat the oven to 180°C/350°F/Gas4
-put the rapeseed oil in a frying pan, add the red onion
and cook on a medium to high heat for 5-10 minutes
until soft and golden brown.
-add the sliced beetroot, oregano and the balsamic
vinegar. Reduce the heat a little and continue to warm
the beetroot through, stirring occassionally for 5 minutes.
Season with salt and pepper. keep warm.
-destalk and tear the kale into small pieces. Toss with the
rapeseed oil, salt and pepper in a bowl.Tip onto a
baking tray and cook in the preheated oven for 10
minutes, turning halfway through, until crispy.
-place the rocket leaves in a salad bowl topped with the
warm beetroot and finally the crsipy kale. Drizzle with a
little more rapeseed oil and balsalmic vinegar if you like.

serves 4 as an accompaniment to a main dish.

Superfoods at their best- to eat on their own or as an accompaniment to a main dish.

Note:
To cook beetroot, top, tail and scrub the beetroot. Take a very large sheet of aluminium cooking foil,
fold in half making sure it's large enough to create a parcel to contain the beetroot. Place the beetroot
on the foil, fold in the sides and top leaving an opening, through which to pour a cm or so of cold
water. Completely seal the foil parcel, place on a tray in a preheated oven at 180°C/350°F/Gas4
for 1 hour and 15 minutes until the beetroot is cooked through. Allow to cool, and then scrape off the
skin with a small knife.

warm salad of roasted aubergine, squash and tomato with spinach and maple toasted pumpkin seeds

ingredients:

method:

1 aubergine, cut into 4cm² chunks
1 small butternut squash, peeled deseeded and cut into 4cm² chunks
rapeseed oil
salt and pepper
100g cherry plum tomatoes

for the maple toasted seeds:
2 tbsp pumpkin seeds
1 tbsp maple syrup
1 tbsp rapeseed oil

to finish:
100g baby leaf spinach
75g Yorkshire Fettle cheese
2 tbsp rapeseed oil
1 tsp fig and orange balsamic vinegar (Yorkshire Drizzle)
salt and pepper

-preheat the oven to 180°C/350°F/Gas4.
-place the aubergine and squash on a roasting tray and drizzle with oil, toss the vegetables in the oil to evenly coat and sprinkle with salt and pepper.
-roast the vegetables in the preheated oven for 20 minutes, add the tomatoes, turn all the veg in the oil again and roast for another 15 minutes until golden and tender.
-whilst the vegetables are cooking, place the pumpkin seeds, oil and maple syrup in a bowl, mix well together and lay out on a baking tray lined with baking parchment. Roast in the oven for 8-10 minutes.
-when the vegetables are cooked, put the spinach in a large serving bowl or plate, add the hot cooked vegetables, toss together, crumble over the Fettle, scatter on the maple toasted seeds and pour over the rapeseed oil and the fig and orange drizzle. Season with a little salt and some freshly ground black pepper and serve whilst still warm.

serves 4 as a starter, 2 as a main course.

A wholesome autumnal feast to eat on its own or to accompany some juicy roasted chicken thighs.

watermelon, pickled onion and feta salad

ingredients:

½ small red onion, cut into thin, half moon slices
2 limes, juiced
1kg watermelon, skin and pips removed
125g feta cheese or Yorkshire Fettle
1 small bunch flat leaf parsley, leaves removed
1 small bunch mint, leaves removed and chopped
black pepper
1 tbsp toasted pumpkin and sunflower seeds (see note)
2 tbsp extra virgin olive oil

method:

-place the onion in a bowl with the lime juice.
-cut the watermelon into 5cm chunks. Cut the feta into cubes, and place both on a large serving platter, add the whole parsley leaves and chopped mint. Grind over some black pepper.
-add the onions and juices. Mix together very lightly. Scatter over the toasted pumpkin and sunflower seeds. Drizzle over the olive oil and serve.

serves 4 as an accompaniment to a main course.

Summertime in a bowl, fabulous with some simple grilled lamb chops.

Note:
To toast pumpkin and sunflower seeds toss a handful of each into a dry frying pan. Cook over a moderate heat, moving the seeds constantly until they start to pop and turn light golden in colour. When cool store in a jam jar.

cajun roasted cauliflower with orange yoghurt dressing

Ingredients:

1 cauliflower, cut into small florets
2 tbsp rapeseed oil
2 tsp Cajun spice recipe (p. 67)
3 tbsp Greek yoghurt
juice and zest of ½ orange
pinch Cajun spice

method:

-preheat the oven to 180°C/350°F/Gas4
-place the cauliflower in a bowl.
-mix the oil and the Cajun spice in a large bowl and toss in the cauliflower, mix well together and place on a roasting tray and roast in the oven for 20 minutes.
-for the orange yoghurt mix together yoghurt, orange juice and zest. Season with salt, pepper and a pinch of Cajun spice.
-serve warm on a platter drizzled with the orange yoghurt.

serves 4 as an accompaniment to a main dish.

Spice up some cauliflower for a great winter salad to eat just as it is or with some grilled sausages.

I have made and demonstrated this dish many times, also used it at the cookery school to teach people a few different skills. It requires making caramel and pastry, two things a lot of people would shy away from, but hopefully if you follow this recipe carefully it will banish those fears!

beetroot tart tatin

ingredients:

method:

for the pastry:
115g plain flour
pinch of salt
75g butter, frozen for at least 2 hours
4-5 tbsp very cold water

for the filling:
2 large sprigs rosemary
75g golden caster sugar
40g butter
1 tsp fig and orange Yorkshire drizzle/balsamic vinegar
1 tbsp runny honey
400g beetroot, cooked (p. 37 note)
1 Camembert or a thick slice of goat's cheese log
salt and pepper

-first make the pastry. the butter needs to be very cold direct from the freezer.
-sift the flour and salt into a mixing bowl.
-dip the frozen butter into the flour, it helps to stop the butter melting in your hand. Grate the frozen butter on the coarse side of the grater into the flour rest the grater the in bowl which helps you to apply more pressure whilst grating. Keep dipping the butter into the flour as needed so it is easier to grate.
-with a palette knife mix the butter into the flour until the mixture is crumbly.
-start with 4 ½ tbsp of the very cold water then stir in to start to bring the dough together. Add the remaining water a little at a time and finally bring the dough together lightly with your hands. Don't make the dough too wet otherwise it becomes impossible to roll out later. It is better for the dough to be on the dry side rather than the wet side.

-shape the pastry into a round flat disc then loosely wrap with cling film, flatten as much as you can into a circle and refrigerate for 30 minutes.
-preheat the oven to 180°C/350°F/Gas4.
-strip the leaves off one of the stalks of rosemary and roughly chop the leaves, keeping the other sprig of rosemary whole.
-place a small heavy ovenproof frying pan over a medium heat. Add the sugar to the pan and wait until it starts to caramelise at the edges, lower the heat a little and stir the undissolved sugar in unitl it all melts and caramelises. Carefully add a large pinch of salt, the butter, vinegar and honey. Remove the pan from the heat and stir until everything is melted together. Add the chopped rosemary and then lay the whole stalk of rosemary over the caramel.
-slice the cooked beetroot into neat 1cm rounds. Lay them carefully and neatly in overlapping spirals on top of the caramel, it will be very hot. Season with salt and pepper.
-lay the cheese on top of the sliced beetroot in the centre of the pan.
-roll out the pastry on a well floured board into a circle large enough to cover the beetroot.
-lay the pastry on top of the beetroot and cheese and tuck the edges in to the pan seal everything in.
-place in the pre-heated oven for 30 minutes until golden brown.
-carefully remove from the oven, remembering that the handle will be very hot. Allow to sit for a couple of minutes, and then gently make a hole at the edge of the pastry and drain away the excess liquid into a small saucepan. Place an upturned plate over the pan. holding the two together, flip over and leave the pan for a few seconds to allow all the caramel to fall away.
-bring the saucepan of drained liquid to the boil and boil rapidly until reduced, take care as it will burn if boiled too long.
-serve whilst still warm with salad and the reduced juices drizzled over.

serves 4 as a starter or light lunch.

People are always afraid of making gluten free pastry, it's actually easy to make but a little more tricky to roll out. With this method, it becomes more manageable and I find that it makes a really good crumbly light pastry. You can of course use traditional shortcrust pastry if you prefer.

asparagus and smoked salmon quiche

ingredients::

for the pastry:
225g gluten free plain flour
100g chilled butter, cubed
1 egg
pinch salt

for the filling:
150ml double cream
2 eggs, beaten
1 bunch of asparagus
4 tsp full fat cream cheese
1 tbsp chopped fresh dill
100g smoked salmon, cut into strips
salt and pepper

method:

-preheat the oven to 170°C/325°F/Gas3.
-first make the pastry. Put the flour and salt into a food processor bowl. Add the cubed butter, process for about 30 seconds until it resembles fine breadcrumbs. With the motor running drop in the egg and continue processing until the dough comes together.
-form into a ball and cut in half. Press both halves out into a flat circle. wrap one half in cling film, this can be frozen up to a month for future use.
-roll out one piece of the pastry between 2 sheets of cling film, to a circle large enough to fill the base of a 20cm flan dish.

-remove the top layer of the cling film, flip the pastry over using the bottom layer of cling film to place into your flan dish, the cling film also makes it easier to push the pastry into the edges and up the sides of the flan dish. When it is completely covered remove the cling film. If you notice any cracks just patch up with the left over pastry.
-whisk the cream and egg for the filling together and season generously.
-prick the pastry all over the bottom of the pie dish with a fork.
-brush the pastry all over with some of the cream and egg mixture and place in the preheated oven on a baking sheet for 10 minutes. Remove from the oven.
-trim the asparagus by snapping the ends off, they will naturally break at the correct place.
-discard the pieces you have snapped off or use to make soup.
-chop the asparagus into lengths long enough to fit your flan case and slice the remainder into 1 cm rounds.
-boil a pan of salted water. Drop all the asparagus into the boiling water and blanch for 1 minute. Drain into a colander and run cold water over the asparagus to cool it down. Place onto some kitchen towel to drain thoroughly.
-put the cream cheese into the bottom of the pastry case and carefully spread it out. Cover with the small pieces of chopped asparagus stalks, and evenly arrange the asparagus stalks and smoked salmon on top then sprinkle with the dill. Pour the remaining cream and egg mixture over the top of everything.
-carefully place in the oven on a baking sheet and bake for 25 minutes until set and golden brown.
-serve with a simple watercress salad.

serves 4 as a starter or light lunch.

mains

maple syrup, soy and ginger salmon with stir fried greens

ingredients:

method:

for the marinade:
25g ginger, peeled and grated
2 tbsp soy sauce
1 tbsp maple syrup
1 tsp sesame oil
1 lime, juice and zest
4 salmon fillets (about 600g)

for the vegetables:
2 tsp sesame oil
200g tenderstem broccoli
100g mange tout
200g pak or bok choi, cut into ¼ lengthways
4 spring onions, white parts only sliced into 3cm
lengths (use the green parts to finish)

for the sauce:
1 tsp cornflour
2 tbsp oyster sauce
1 tbsp dark soy sauce
1 tbsp chinese cooking wine
1 cloves garlic, finely chopped
1 tbsp rapeseed oil
½ tsp caster sugar
5g fresh ginger, peeled and cut into matchsticks

to finish:
½ tsp sesame seeds
green parts 4 spring onions, finely sliced

-mix together the ginger, soy sauce, maple syrup, sesame oil, lime juice and zest in a shallow container and add the salmon fillets making sure they are well covered. leave to marinate for 1- 4 hours.
-preheat the oven to 180°C/350°F/Gas4.
-remove the salmon from the marinade, keep the marinade for later.
-heat a frying pan to high, brown the salmon on both sides, then pour over the reserved marinade and place in the oven for 10 minutes.
-whilst the salmon is cooking, bring a large pan of water to the boil and add 1 tsp of sesame oil.
-drop in the tenderstem broccoli and when the water comes back to the boil count to 20 then lift the broccolli out with a slotted spoon into a colander and run cold water over the broccoli until it is cool. Place on a kitchen paper lined tray to drain.
-repeat the process with the mange tout. Then set aside the vegetables.
-mix together the sauce ingredients in a small bowl.
-heat a wok to a high temperature and add the sauce mixture.
-cook for a minute or so to heat up then add the pak choi, stir fry for 2 minutes then add the cooked broccoli and mange tout. Continue to stir fry until the vegetables are all warmed through.
-remove the salmon from the oven taking care with the pan handle as it will be hot, take the salmon out of the pan and keep warm. If the juices are very liquid in the pan, place it back on the heat and reduce until the liquid becomes glossy.

-put the vegetables on a plate with a piece of salmon on top, drizzle with the sauce and sprinkle over the sesame seeds and spring onions.

serves 4.

A simple way to pimp up your salmon fillet. Not only does it look good but tastes great too. I love pairing fish with oriental flavours, they really complement both light white fish and the more robust oily ones too.

tuna with mango and papaya salsa

ingredients:

450g fresh tuna cut into four equal steaks
rapeseed oil
½ ripe mango, peeled, destoned and finely diced
½ ripe papaya, peeled, deseeded and finely diced
1 red chilli, deseeded and finely chopped
60 ml white wine vinegar
60g caster sugar
1 ½ tbsp of water
55g washed rocket leaves
10g fresh coriander, leaves only

method:

-combine the vinegar, sugar and water into a pan and stir until sugar has dissolved.
-bring to the boil and cook uncovered for 3 minutes.
-put the chopped mango, papaya and chilli in a bowl and then pour the cooked syrup over the fruit and set aside.
-remove the tuna from the fridge an hour before you intend to cook it. This means that you can cook the tuna very quickly so it's still very rare in the middle but not stone cold. Season the tuna steaks with sea salt and drizzle with the rapeseed oil, rubbing them into the fish.
-heat a large frying pan to a high heat. When very hot add the tuna steaks and sear until golden brown, carefully turn and repeat on the other side. Each side should only take about a minute.
-divide the rocket and coriander stalks between four plates and place a tuna steak on top of the rocket. Place a little of the salsa on top of each steak and drizzle the remainder around the side of the plate over the rocket and coriander.
-serve straight away.

serves 4.

This dish I ate at the Crab and Lobster, one of my Mum's favourite restaurants. We had a wonderful family celebration of her 70th birthday there. They did this as a starter, I have made it both as a starter, for lunch or as a canapé served on Chinese spoons.

stir fried tiger prawns with thai basil

ingredients:

2 tbsp ground nut/vegetable oil
2 cloves garlic, chopped
1 red chilli, finely chopped
1 small cooking onion, halved and finely sliced
10 large raw peeled prawns, de-veined
1 tsp palm sugar or light soft brown sugar
2 tbsp fish sauce
1 tbsp dark soy sauce
10g fresh Thai basil (or 2 tbsp dried) leaves stripped and chopped

method:

-heat a wok until smoking and add the oil.
-fry the garlic, chilli and onion over a moderate heat for 1 minute.
-turn up the heat and tip in the prawns and (if using the dried thai basil add at this point, if using fresh add at the end of the recipe). Stir-fry for 2-3 minutes until the prawns have turned pink. Add the palm sugar and stir fry for 30 seconds.
-add the fish sauce and soy sauce, then cook for a further 30 seconds.
-remove from the heat and stir in the fresh thai basil.
-serve with fragrant jasmine rice.

serves 2 as a starter/1 as a main course

This is the first of two prawn stir fries. after having lived in Hong Kong I can't get enough of Asian flavours. It opened up a whole new world to me. Thai style food is my favourite to cook, it usually requires quite a bit of pre-preparation, but cooks in a flash.

Note:
Thai basil available online, some Waitrose, Sainsburys and Morrisons stores, and Rafters of Driffield will get it for you with prior notice. If you cant find Thai basil, use normal basil, it's not the same, but will still taste good.

fragrant jasmine rice

ingredients:

110g jasmine rice washed thoroughly
1 thumb ginger sliced
1 stalk lemongrass crushed
1 lime leaf
1 spring onion, finely chopped
600ml hot water
salt

method:

-to make a fragrant stock in which to cook the rice, bring the water to the boil slowly with the lemongrass, ginger, lime leaf and spring onions.
-very gently simmer for 10 minutes.
-strain into a jug.
-put the washed rice into a saucepan and strain over enough of the liquid to just cover plus 2cm extra.
-bring to the boil, add some salt, cover and reduce the heat to the bare minimum and cook very gently for 10-12 minutes until all the stock is absorbed. If necessary add a little more stock if the rice is still hard.
-check the rice is cooked, fluff with a fork and serve immediately.

serves 2

tamarind prawns

ingredients:

for the sauce:
2 tsp tamarind paste
15g palm sugar or light soft brown sugar
2 tbsp hot water
2 tbsp fish sauce
¼ tsp cayenne pepper

for the stir fry:
1 tbsp coconut oil
10 large raw peeled prawns
½ red pepper, deseeded and cut into 1x4cm strips
2 cloves garlic, peeled and crushed (see p. 131)
1 small piece galangal, finely chopped (see note)
½ red chilli, finely chopped
10g fresh thai basil (or 2 tbsp dried) leaves stripped and chopped (see p. 55 note)
10g fresh coriander, chopped

method:

-to make the sauce mix together the tamarind and palm sugar, stir in the hot water to dissolve the sugar. Add the fish sauce and cayenne pepper and stir well together.
-place the red pepper in a bowl with 2 tbsp of the sauce.
-pat the prawns dry and place in a bowl and coat with the remainder of the sauce.
-heat a wok until smoking and add the coconut oil.
-fry the garlic, galangal and chilli over a moderate heat for 1 minute. Add the red pepper and stir-fry for 2-3 minutes.
-turn up the heat and tip in the prawns with all of the sauce. if using the dried basil, add at this stage. Stir-fry for 2-3 minutes until the prawns have turned pink.
-remove from the heat and stir in the fresh herbs.
-serve with fragrant jasmine rice (p. 55).

serves 2 as a starter/1 as a main course

Another thai style prawn dish, tamarind imparts a tangy sour flavour that sets your taste buds alight. This dish can also be made with diced chicken thigh fillets, it will just take a bit longer to cook.

Note:
Galangal is usually available from oriental supermarkets. If you can't find galangal, use fresh ginger instead.

fresh pasta

ingredients:

200g '00' or pasta flour
2 large eggs
1 tbsp water
a large pinch of salt
semolina flour for dusting

method:

-sift the flour and salt onto your work surface. Make a large well in the centre of the flour, break in the eggs, and add the water.
-break up the eggs and beat together with a fork. Keep beating with the fork to gradually work in the flour. Continue beating the flour into the egg mixure with the fork until it becomes quite stiff. Then quickly work in the remaining flour by chopping it into the egg and flour paste in the centre.

-using clean hands, work it all together to make a coarse dough. If it is really wet add some more flour, or if dry a little water.
-then knead the dough. If you have a machine put the dough into a lightly floured bowl and using the dough hook set it going slowly. Knead for 5 minutes until you have a smooth, elastic and workable dough. Rest for 15-30 minutes on the work surface covered by a cloth.
-if you need to do the kneading by hand, flour your work surface and pull one side of the dough towards you with your finger tips, then push away with your knuckles or the palm of your hands, rest as above, 15-30 minutes.
-when ready to use, cut the dough into 3 pieces. Work with one piece at a time leaving the other two covered. Shape into a rectangle and roll out into an even rectangular shape with a rolling pin. Set up the pasta machine and starting on the widest setting, roll the dough through dusted with semolina flour so that it doesn't stick. Fold the pasta into three and roll through again. Repeat this 5 times, dusting with the semolina flour each time until you have a really smooth and well shaped piece of pasta dough.
-turn the machine down 1 notch thinner and roll through again, dusting between each rolling.
-continue working back through the settings of the machine getting thinner each time until you achieve the thickness that you want, usually the 2nd to last for lasagne and ravioli, and the last for tagliatelle and spaghetti.
-cut the pasta through the machine or by hand as required.
-have a large pan of water boiling ready, use 1 litre of water to 110g of pasta and 2 tsp of salt.
-when ready to cook drop in the pasta. Stir occasionally to stop it from sticking, tagliatelle or spaghetti take 2-3 minutes. Drain but always keep some of the cooking water to add to your sauce.

enough for 4 people.

There's always a debate about whether it's worth it to make your own pasta. Some dishes are just right with it, others you can't beat dried. My friend Francesca taught me how to roll out pasta correctly, she was taught by her mum and her mum taught her mum and so on. There's no arguing with a Nonna, so this is definitely the right way! Give it a go, most of us have a pasta machine gathering dust, its great fun, quite therapeutic and a good one to get children involved in. For the best home-made pasta dough the ingredients are one large egg for every 100g flour. You may need to add more flour sometimes, or equally a little more water, as some flours absorb liquid differently, what you need to achieve is a dough which has been kneaded until it is perfectly smooth and elastic, but firm.

Semolina flour is available online on melburyandappleton.co.uk, it's completely different from normal semolina as it's ground much finer.

salmon and prawn ravioli with lemon mascarpone

ingredients:

1 quantity pasta dough (p. 59)

for the filling:
50g smoked salmon
75g cooked peeled king prawns, chopped
25ml double cream
5g fresh dill, finely chopped, stalks and all
freshly ground black pepper
1 egg for sealing
semolina flour (see pg. 59)

for the sauce:
½ lemon juiced
80g mascarpone cheese
5g dill, chopped
grated parmesan

method:

-lightly whip the double cream in a bowl. Roughly chop the remainder of the salmon and add to the prawns along with the chopped prawns and the dill. Season well with black pepper. Chill well.
-divide the pasta dough into 3 pieces, shape into a rectangle and roll out into an even rectangular shape with a rolling pin. When ready to use, cut the dough into 3 pieces. Work with one piece at a time leaving the other two covered. Set up the pasta machine and starting on the widest setting, roll the dough through dusted with semolina flour so that it doesn't stick. Fold the pasta into three and roll through again. Repeat this 5 times, dusting with the semolina flour each time until you have a really smooth and well shaped piece of pasta dough.
-turn the machine down 1 notch thinner and roll through again, dusting between each rolling. Continue working back through the settings of the machine getting thinner every time until the second to last setting on the machine.

-lay the pasta sheet on a work surface well dusted with semolina flour and cut the pasta strip in half. On one half spoon a teaspoon of filling onto the pasta at 5 cm intervals leaving 5 cm at each end free.
-brush all around the filling with beaten egg and very carefully lay the other half of the pasta over the top of the filling sealing round three sides, on the fourth side try to get out all of the air before sealing. Cut around the pasta with a fluted pasta cutter. set aside on a tray dusted well with semolina flour. repeat with the remaining pasta.
-when ready to cook boil a very large pan of water with 1 tsp of salt. Place in the ravioli and cook for 2-3 minutes, or until the ravioli rises to the top of the water. Keep warm and retain some of the cooking water.
-in a frying pan warm through the mascarpone with lemon juice and dill, add 3 tbsp of the pasta cooking water and mix well to make a smooth sauce, bring to a simmer and add the cooked ravioli, add a little more water if you require a thinner sauce.
-serve with some grated parmesan.

serves 2 as a main course or 4 as a starter.

This is a good intro into making your own ravioli. My friend Francesca showed me her way of doing it, it requires a fluted roller to cut the pasta, if you can't find one use a pizza cutter.

thai green chicken curry

ingredients:

method:

for the curry paste:
1 bunch of spring onions, cleaned and roughly chopped
juice and zest of 1 lime
2 green chillies, deseeded and chopped
2 stalks of lemongrass, tough outer layers removed and finely slice the soft centre of the lemongrass (see p. 131)
6 dried lime leaves, soaked in boiling water or use defrosted lime leaves, remove the stalk, chop finely
1 thumb of fresh ginger, peeled and chopped
1 tbsp of fish sauce
1 tbsp of groundnut oil
1 tsp of palm sugar or light soft brown sugar
1 x 15g packet of coriander, leaves stripped and saved for serving, stalks chopped

for the curry:
4 chicken breast fillets
1 tbsp groundnut oil
1 tbsp fish sauce
1 tsp of palm sugar or light soft brown sugar
1 x 400ml can of coconut milk

-put all of the curry paste ingredients into a blender with coriander stalks only, saving the leaves for garnish. Process until smooth. If you don't own a blender you will need to chop all of the paste ingredients much finer and then make the paste in a pestle and mortar. Start with the coarsest ingredients first i.e the ginger, lime leaves and lemongrass, followed by the spring onions, chilli and lime zest. Then add the palm sugar, fish sauce, lime juice and oil.
-chop the chicken breast into large bite size pieces.
-heat a wok until smoking and add the remaining tablespoon of oil.
-fry 2 or more tablespoons of the curry paste, dependant on taste, for 2 minutes. (any unused curry paste can be kept refrigerated for up to a week, or frozen for a month).
-add the fish sauce and palm sugar.
-add the chicken pieces and stir-fry quickly until opaque.
-add the coconut milk, bring to the boil and then reduce the heat.
-simmer curry for 5-10 minutes dependent on the size of your chicken pieces.
-serve with jasmine rice (p. 55) and garnish with reserved coriander leaves.

serves 4

Another Thai style dish. this is my version of the great Thai green curry. I hope you like it, it's quite mild so if you want more heat, increase the amount of chillies, or use birds eye chillies instead.

Save the lemongrass outer leaves for lemongrass and ginger tea (p. 123) , or for jasmine rice stock (p. 55).

chicken thighs stuffed with sausage meat and wrapped in bacon

ingredients:

2 tbsp rapeseed oil
1 small onion, peeled and finely chopped
2 stalks celery, washed and finely chopped
2 stalks lemongrass, tough outer leaves
discarded, finely chopped (see p. 131)
450g best sausage meat you can find!
2 tsp fennel seeds
10g lemon thyme, leaves stripped and chopped
8 boned and skinless chicken thighs
16 slices smoked streaky bacon
500ml medium cider
1 tbsp plain flour
2 tbsp red currant jelly

method:

-preheat the oven to 180°C/350°F/Gas4.
-put the rapeseed oil in a large frying pan and heat to a
medium level, add the chopped onion, celery,
lemongrass, fennel seeds and lemon thyme.
-cook gently for 5 minutes. Allow to cool.
-add the cooled vegetables to the sausage meat and mix
well together. Form into 8 sausage shapes.
-lay out the chicken thighs on a chopping board and
season with salt and pepper, place a sausage of stuffing
on each thigh and close the meat around it.
-stretch the streaky bacon out on a chopping board using
a knife drawing along it to make it as long as possible.
Wrap each thigh in two slices of bacon and secure with
a cocktail stick. Brown the thighs in a dry frying pan and
then transfer to a roasting dish, place in the preheated
oven for 40 minutes.

-remove the chicken from the oven, and keep warm.
-pour off most of the fat from the roasting tin. Keep the juices and add the flour. Mix in well then add the cider.
Place the pan over a medium heat on the hob and whisk to make a gravy, add the red currant jelly, whisk until
dissolved.
-slice the thighs in two diagonally and serve with the hot gravy, sweet potato wedges (p. 87) and some greens.

substantial serving for 4 or lighter portion for 8.

What can beat a sausage, chicken and bacon combo? My sons have always loved a roast chicken
dinner, so I put this together to combine the lot. Make up a batch and freeze, ready for when the
ravenous arrive home.

cajun chicken with winter slaw and sweet potato wedges

ingredients:

method:

for the Cajun spice:
2 tsp sweet paprika
1 ½ tsp garlic powder
1 ½ tsp dried thyme
½ tsp dried basil
½ tsp dried oregano
½ tsp ground black pepper
½ tsp cayenne pepper

for the chicken:
1 tbsp rapeseed oil
600g chicken thigh fillets

for the dressing:
60ml cider vinegar
50g caster sugar
1 tbsp rapeseed oil
1 clove garlic, crushed
¼ tsp fennel seeds, lightly toasted in a dry frying pan
½ tsp salt
black pepper

for the salad:
½ of a small red cabbage, core removed and very finely sliced
1 small fennel bulb, trimmed, cut in half lengthways and finely sliced
1 small red onion, peeled, halved and very finely sliced
10g flat leaf parsley, leaves stripped and roughly chopped
10g fresh coriander, roughly chopped
salt and pepper

-heat an oven to 180°C/350°F/Gas4.
-put all the ingredients for the spice mix into a spice grinder, or pestle and mortar. Process until smooth.
-coat each chicken thigh evenly with half a teaspoon of Cajun spice.
-heat 1 tbsp of rapeseed oil in a frying pan and cook the chicken thighs over a medium to high heat for about 1 minute on each side, and then place in the preheated oven for 20 minutes until cooked through.
-for the salad, place all the ingredients for the dressing in a jam jar and shake well together.
-mix together the vegetables and when ready to serve, pour over the dressing and taste to season.
-serve the cooked chicken in slices with the slaw and sweet potato wedges (p. 87).

serves 4.

the chicken can be substituted for salmon, tuna, lamb or pork steaks.cooking time will need to be adjusted.

Cajun spices really hit the spot, I had Cajun everything in Louisiana including "Gator", whilst I was there though I really could have done with this winter slaw to cleanse the palate. I have pan-fried then baked the chicken as opposed to deep frying, a healthier option. If you want to reduce the sugar in the dressing for a healthier version, give it a try. I have included a recipe for Cajun spice, but of course supermarket bought is also fine.

brined pork chops with mustard honey and cider sauce

ingredients:

method:

for the chops:
2 large pork chops, bone in
2 bay leaves
2 stalks rosemary
6 sprigs thyme
1 sprig sage
8 juniper berries
2 large strips orange peel
500ml water
40g salt
40g caster sugar
30g butter

for the sauce:
200ml medium dry cider
1 tbsp honey
1 tbsp grainy mustard

-place the bay leaves, rosemary, thyme, sage, juniper berries and orange peel in a saucepan with $1/3$ of the water. Bring to the boil then add the salt and sugar. Stir well to dissolve. Allow to cool a little and add the remaining water.
-when cool to the touch, pour the contents of the pan over the pork chops and cover with cling film.
-refrigerate for 2-3 hours dependant on the thickness of the chops.
-when ready to eat, heat the oven to 200°C/375°F/ Gas5.
-remove the chops from the pan and keep warm.
-melt the butter in an ovenproof frying pan, add the herbs from the brine and the pork chops, cook briefly until brown on the underside. Turn over and place in the oven for 10 minutes.
-remove the chops from the oven and keep warm. taking great care because the handle will be hot, place the frying pan on the hob and over a high heat add the cider. Reduce by $2/3$. Add the honey and mustard, stir in. Cook a little more if too runny.
-serve the chops with the sauce, crushed new and sweet potatoes (p. 87), crispy kale (p. 85), and roasted cauliflower (p. 85).

serves 2.

Brining has become all the rage, done a lot in North America, but one that we shy away from as we don't want to eat too much salt. I tried it and I really think it works well with these chops. It also reheats beautifully too.

slow cooked lamb shanks with dates and tamarind

ingredients:

4 lamb shanks
2 tbsp rapeseed oil
2 red onions, peeled and cut into wedges
6 cloves garlic, peeled
2 carrots, peeled and grated
110ml red wine
2 sprigs rosemary
1 small red chilli, deseeded and sliced
40ml balsamic vinegar
40ml soy sauce
110ml tamarind paste
vegetable stock
170g pitted dates, roughly chopped

method:

-preheat the oven to 170°C/340°F/Gas3
-brown the lamb shanks in 1 tbsp of the rapeseed oil in a deep casserole dish. Remove and keep warm.
-lightly brown the onions and garlic with the remaining oil, return the lamb to the pan, add the wine and bring to the boil.
-add the remaining ingredients, except for the dates, with enough stock to cover and place in the oven for 2 hours.
-remove from the oven, skim as much fat as you can from the top, then add the dates. Return to the oven for 20 minutes. skim the fat off again if necessary.
-serve with roasted vegetables (p. 83) and some crisp green beans.

serves 4

A good few years ago I did a "Stage" at the great Peter Gordon's restaurant, The Providores on Marylebone High Street. His kitchen is in a very hot basement, and it ran like clockwork, everyone worked seamlessly together, no raised voices and excellent food. this is my version of one of his recipes, tamarind coming to the fore again, beautifully offsetting the richness of lamb. Be hungry for this one!

beef cheek ragu with porcini mushrooms and pappardelle

ingredients:

35g dried porcini mushrooms
300ml beef stock (see note)
2 beef cheeks (approx 800g)
2 tbsp olive oil
2 sticks celery, washed and diced
2 small red onions, finely chopped
4 stalks rosemary, leaves removed and finely chopped
2 bay leaves
1 clove garlic, sliced
1 400g can chopped tomatoes
185ml full bodied red wine
1 tbsp tomato puree
1 quantity of basic pasta dough (p. 59)
salt and pepper
50g freshly grated parmesan

method:

-preheat the oven to 150°C/300°F/Gas2.
-place the porcini mushrooms in a saucepan and add the beef stock, bring to the boil and turn off the heat. Leave to soak.
-heat a non-stick frying pan over a high heat and add a tablespoon of olive oil, when very hot brown the beef cheeks and then transfer to a plate.
-add the remaining oil to the frying pan and cook the celery, onion, rosemary and bay leaves, over a lower heat, to soften the vegetables for 10 minutes. Add the sliced garlic and cook for just a minute. Add to the casserole dish.
-turn up the heat on the frying pan and deglaze the pan with a little of the red wine, scraping all the goodness off the bottom of the pan. Turn off the heat and add to the casserole dish.

-strain the stock from the mushrooms through a fine sieve into the casserole. Rinse the mushrooms with water to remove any grit and add them to the casserole. Bring the contents of the casserole to the boil, and reduce the liquid by half, this will take about 5-8 minutes.
-add the tinned tomatoes, remaining red wine, tomato puree and browned beef cheeks. Bring to the boil. Cover the contents of the pan with a circle of baking parchment, put the lid on and place in the preheated oven for 2½ - 3 hours until the meat is very tender. Shred the meat using 2 forks. Season to taste.
-roll out the pasta as per the recipe on page 59, when you have got to large sheets at the thickness for lasagne, dust well with semolina flour, and fold into four. Cut the pasta into 3cm thick ribbons, using a pasta cutter and a rolling pin to keep you straight.
-bring a large pan of water to the boil with 1 tsp salt.
-drop in the pasta and cook for 3 minutes. Drain through a colander, keeping some of the cooking water to loosen the casserole sauce if necessary.
-mix the casserole and pasta together carefully and add some of the water if it needs more sauce. Taste for seasoning.
-serve with some freshly grated parmesan.

serves 4.

My neighbour Alison Sutcliffe produces excellent home reared beef. She goes out of her way to get you what you want and having worked in the catering trade knows exactly what cooks and chefs want. This dish made with her beef cheeks is finger licking good. Try to make your own pasta, if thats a bridge too far use a thick dried pasta or serve with some creamy mash, leaving the beef in larger chunks.

Note:
Most supermarkets now sell ambient pouches of liquid beef stock ready to use. These are much better than the cubes or powder as they are much less salty.

73

tagliata di manzo

ingredients:

for the steak:
2 x 225g sirloin steaks about 2.5cm/1 inch thick at room temperature
2 tbsp rapeseed oil for brushing the steaks
sea salt and black pepper
2 cloves garlic, crushed with the skin on
2 stalks rosemary, leaves stripped and finely chopped
juice and zest of ½ lemon
60ml rapeseed oil
30g bag rocket, washed and dried

method:

-remove the steaks from the fridge and allow to come to room temperature.
-brush the steaks with 1 tbsp of oil and season well.
-heat a large frying pan until very hot.
-sear the steaks on each side for 2 minutes (rare), 3-4 minutes (medium), 5-6 minutes (well done).
-remove from the pan and allow to rest in a warm place for 5-10 minutes whilst you prepare the salad.
-add the remaining rapeseed oil to the frying pan and turn down to a medium heat.
-add the garlic cloves, rosemary and lemon zest. Cook for 3 minutes and add the lemon juice.
-divide the rocket between two plates. Strain over half of the sauce.
-put the steaks on a chopping board and carve into thick slices, keeping each steak together. Place each steak on top of the rocket and pour over the remaining sauce.

serves 2

We have travelled a lot around italy in the last 12 years, and this is always a go to dish. The best I have tasted was at Ristorante Fragana, on Isola di San Pietro in Sardinia. Very simple to do but this is all about the ingredients so it's important to get a good quality steak and to rest after cooking.

Back to Thai style food here, one for the spring time when the fabulous aspargus comes into season. In Yorkshire we are blessed with many top quality growers, and you really can taste the difference from imported.

stir fried beef with oyster sauce and asparagus

ingredients:

175g asparagus
2 tbsp ground nut/vegetable oil
2 cloves garlic, finely chopped
175g lean rump steak
2 tbsp oyster sauce
1 tbsp fish sauce
½ tsp palm sugar or light soft brown sugar
¼ tsp ground white pepper
2 spring onions, sliced
½ tsp of sesame seeds

method:

-trim the asparagus by snapping the ends off, they will naturally break at the correct place.
-discard the pieces you have snapped off or use to make soup.
-cut the asparagus into 5cm lengths.
-bring a pan of water to the boil and add the asparagus. When the water comes back to the boil count to 20. Pour the asparagus into a colander and run cold water over it until it has cooled right down. Place some kitchen paper on a plate and lay out the asparagus on it to drain.
-trim any fat off the steak and cut into thin slices across the grain.
-heat a wok over a high heat until it is very hot and add the groundnut oil, and garlic. Cook for 30 seconds.
-add the beef slices and stir fry for about 2 minutes until it is lightly browned.
-add the oyster sauce, fish sauce, sugar, pepper and asparagus and stir fry until the asparagus has warmed through.
-turn onto a serving plate and sprinkle with the spring onions and sesame seeds.

serves 2

My Mum really was the most fantastic cook, totally self taught and through a lot of disasters (mainly palmed off on my Uncle Snuff who would eat anything) she rose to be one of the best cooks I have ever known. Her stews were legendary, here I have modernised it a bit with short rib, but it makes beautifully with stewing steak too. If you use stewing steak, get it cut a bit bigger than usual, it's easier to brown and makes a great pie filling. and the pastry from the beetroot tart tatin (p. 45) recipe makes a really good, crispy, pie pastry.

Burton's Butchers in Pocklington supply fabulous Gibendale prime beef, well worth seeking out.

beer braised beef short rib

ingredients:

100g bacon lardons
4 beef short ribs (about 300g each)
rapeseed oil
2 sticks celery, washed and diced
1 small cooking onion, peeled and roughly chopped
1 carrot, peeled and diced
1 500ml bottle dark beer such as Wold Top
Shepherd's Watch
2 tbsp plain flour
2 stalks thyme
1 bay leaf
8 small shallots, peeled and kept whole
110g button chestnut mushrooms, washed
30g butter
2 tbsp demerara sugar
2 tbsp brandy

method:

-preheat the oven to 140°C/275°F/Gas2
-heat a non-stick frying pan over a high heat and brown the bacon lardons without adding any oil. Keep the bacon fat in the frying pan, scoop out the lardons and place in a casserole dish. Brown the short ribs in the reserved bacon fat, adding a little more oil if necessary, when they are a lovely golden brown, remove from the pan and set to one side.
-then brown the celery, carrot and onion with a little more oil if necessary, add to the casserole dish. Deglaze the pan with a little beer, scraping all the goodnes from the bottom.
-add the flour to the vegetables and stir to coat everything. Then add the beer from the deglazed pan and the remaining beer, stir well together. Add the browned short ribs and bring to simmering point on the hob.
-make a little bundle of the thyme and bay leaf and tie with string. Add to the casserole. Cover with the lid and transfer to the preheated oven and cook for 2 ½ hours.

-whilst the casserole is cooking, melt half of the butter and half of the sugar in a small frying pan and add the shallots, cook over a moderate to high heat until caramelised, transfer to a dish. Repeat with the remaining sugar, butter and mushrooms. When the mushrooms are cooked, add the brandy and bubble furiously to deglaze the pan. Add to the shallots.
-after 2 ½ hours of cooking time check the beef to see if it is tender, if it is coming away from the bone then add the onions and mushrooms and cook for another ½ hour in the oven, if not cook a little longer before adding the mushrooms and shallots.
-serve with leek and potato mash (p. 87) and some roasted vegetables (p. 83).

serves 4-6 depending on the size of the short ribs.

vegetables

roasted vegetables

3 tbsp smoked rapeseed oil (see suppliers)
250g white potato, or sweet potato scrubbed and cut into chunks
1 carrot, peeled and chopped into thick batons
125g swede, peeled and cut into chunks
½ butternut squash, peeled and deeseeded and cut into chunks
1 parsnip, peeled and cut into thick batons
3 stalks thyme
5 cloves garlic, bashed

method

-preheat the oven to 200°C/400°F/Gas5
-in an ovenproof pan, heat the smoked oil and quickly brown the potato, carrot, swede, butternut squash, and parsnip. Add the thyme and garlic and place in the preheated oven for 45 minutes, turning them over after 30 minutes of cooking.

serves 4

I have put here a selection of winter veg, but in the summer you can use courgettes, peppers, new potatoes, cherry tomatoes and anything else you fancy. Try and source smoked rapeseed oil from Yorkshire rapeseed oil.

braised savoy cabbage

ingredients:

400g savoy cabbage
25g butter
¼ tsp vegetable stock powder
100ml boiling water
ground black pepper

method:

-peel off the outer leaves of the cabbage, cut in half and remove the central core.
-slice the cabbage into 3mm slices.
-melt the butter in a casserole dish, large enough to fit the cabbage in, over a medium heat, add the vegetable stock powder and water.
-add the cabbage, stir well to coat with the buttery water then place the lid on, reduce the heat to medium low and cook for 10-15 minutes, stirring occasionally, until the cabbage is cooked to your liking.

serves 4

This is a simple recipe but a winner every time. really buttery, delicious cabbage leaves leaving boiled cabbage as a horrible distant memory!

crispy kale

ingredients:

200g curly kale, preferably on the stalk
2 tbsp rapeseed oil
salt and pepper

method:

-preheat the oven to 180°C/350°F/Gas4
-remove the stalk from the kale and wash well.
-dry on kitchen paper and then tear the kale into 5cm squarish pieces and put in a bowl.
-toss with the oil and salt and pepper.
-lay on a baking sheet, in a single layer, you may need to use two.
-cook in the oven for 10 minutes, turning after 5 minutes.
-if you want to add spices, toss in with the kale and oil before cooking, you can add cumin, coriander, chilli, smoked paprika, whatever you fancy.

serves 4 as part of a selection of vegetables.

Crispy kale is a sure fire hit of a vegetable, particularly if you love a bit of salt like me, one of my Mum's only vices that I inherited. Roasting cauliflower brings out a lovely nuttiness in it, add different spices to suit the dish you are cooking, or eat the cauliflower as a dish in itself.

roasted cauliflower

ingredients:

1 large cauliflower, trimmed with leaves removed and cut into 4 x 4cm slices, use the trimmings and outside pieces for soup or cauliflower couscous or rice
40g butter melted

2 rapeseed oil
¼ tsp each of: ground allspice, cumin, coriander and smoked paprika
salt and pepper

method:

-preheat the oven to 180°C/350°F/Gas4
-melt the butter with the oil and spices in a frying pan and cook gently until the butter starts to brown.
-place the slices of cauliflower on a roasting tray and drizzle over the spicy brown butter. Turn the cauliflower over making sure each side is coated in the butter.
-place in the preheated oven and roast for 40 minutes, basting occassionally with the butter.
-serve immediately.

serves 4 as part of a selection of vegetables.

crushed new and sweet potatoes

ingredients:

300g new potatoes, washed
300g sweet potatoes, peeled and chopped into large chunks
2 tbsp rapeseed
salt and pepper

method:

-in a covered large saucepan, boil the new and sweet potatoes in salted water until tender, about 15-20 minutes.
-drain the potatoes and put back into the saucepan, season with salt and pepper and add the rapseed oil.
-crush them roughly with the back of a fork and stir to mix in the oil and seasonings.

serves 4.

After the deliciousness of the first new potatoes of the season, I'm constantly thinking of new ways to vary new potato dishes. Add, for instance, some chopped spring onions cooked in butter or oil for a lovely accompaniment to fish.

leek and potato mash

ingredients:

600g potatoes (preferably King Edward or Estima)
200g leeks, washed, and thinly sliced
30g butter
100ml full fat milk
¼ tsp salt
freshly ground black pepper

method:

-peel and chop the potatoes into smallish chunks.
-place in a steamer over a pan of simmering water, cook for 20 minutes or until tender (see p. 131).
-heat the butter and milk together in a small shallow pan, add the sliced leeks and simmer gently for 10 minutes until just cooked.
-push the cooked potatoes through a ricer or mash, and add the milky leeks. Mix thoroughly.
-check for seasoning.

serves 4.

spicy sweet potato wedges

ingredients:

2 sweet potatoes scrubbed and cut into wedges
olive or rapeseed oil
1 tsp smoked paprika
¼ tsp ground cumin

method:

-preheat the oven to 200°C/400°F/Gas6
-tip the sweet potatoes into a roasting tin and drizzle with oil, scatter over the spices, toss to coat the potatoes and place in the pre-heated oven for 30 minutes, turn the potatoes over and cook for a further 15 minutes until tender and golden.

serves 2-3

You can mix up the spices to your taste adding chilli to give a dish a bigger kick if you prefer.

desserts

orange liqueur pannacotta with raspberry and orange

ingredients:

method:

for the pannacotta:
2 ½ gelatine leaves
200ml double cream
150ml full fat milk
25g caster sugar
3 tbsp orange liqueur (Drambuie or Raisthorpe orange liqueur)

for the raspberry and orange compote:
225g raspberries
30g caster sugar
grated rind ½ orange
2 tbsp freshly squeezed orange juice

-soak the gelatine leaves in a bowl of cold water for 5 minutes until soft .
-put the cream, milk and sugar into a saucepan and warm to hand hot, enough to dissolve the sugar.
-squeeze the water out of the gelatine leaves and drop them into the cream. Stir to dissolve. Add the liqueur and mix in well.
-divide the mixture between the 4x150ml dariole moulds, ramekins or glass dishes, if you prefer. Chill for 3-4 hours until set (or overnight).
-next place 110g raspberries in a bowl with the caster sugar, orange zest and juice. Crush with a fork and then pass through a sieve. Chill until required.

-to serve, dip the moulds briefly in boiling water, turn onto a plate, serve with the remainder of raspberries and the raspberry and orange sauce around the pannacottas.
-on the picture, I have served with confit of orange zest. To make this pare the zest off 4 oranges, bring a small pan of water to the boil, drop in the orange zest and cook for 5 minutes, then strain through a sieve. Put 100g caster sugar in a small pan add 100ml of boiling water and stir to dissolve over a low heat. Bring to the boil and simmer for 3 minutes, add the cooked orange zest and continue to simmer until the syrup thickens. Pour the contents into a jar and use the sticky orange zest to garnish the pannacotta. You can do the same with the zest from any citrus fruit.

serves 4.

Pannacotta is my usual choice of dessert in Italy, it's so simple to make and you can dress it up no end to look fabulous. Flavours can be changed easily, try infusing with ginger and serving with a rhubarb compote. Try to locate cream and full fat milk from my friends Pete and Sarah Burdass at St Quintin's Creamery. Using full fat milk for cooking makes such a difference, and as Pete will tell you full fat milk is 96% fat free!

This is a quick, easy dessert to whip up using either bags of frozen fruit, or a mixture of fruit that's lurking in your freezer. If there is any coulis left over, it is delicious with yoghurt and fresh fruit for a breakfast treat.

berry bavarois with fruit coulis

ingredients:

method:

250 ml fresh berry pulp, made from 450g of assorted berries
70g icing sugar
2 gelatine leaves
3 tbsp boiling water
150 ml greek style yoghurt
250 ml double cream, lightly whipped
a handful of mixed raspberries, strawberries and blueberries
4x 150ml dariole moulds, ramekins or serving glasses

-begin by blending the berries and icing sugar in a food processor or blender and then push through a fine sieve using a ladle to help you push as much of the fruit puree through as possible, leaving only the seeds.
-soak the leaf gelatine in cold water for 5 minutes. Place 3 tablespoons of boiling water in a jug, squeeze the water out of the soaked geletine and drop into hot water to dissolve it.
-place the dissolved gelatine, half of the berry puree and yoghurt in a food processor or blender and puree for 1 minute.
-tip into a large bowl and gently fold in the whipped cream.

-pour into the moulds or serving dishes as quickly as you can because it will start to set almost straight away.
-chill for at least 2 hours.
-if using the dariole moulds, dip briefly into very hot water and turn out onto a plate and drizzle with a little of the remaining fruit coulis and some extra berries as a garnish, or serve in the ramekin or glass dish with coulis and berries on the top,in both instances it's a must to have a hazelnut and orange biscuit (p. 115) on the side.

serves 4

Another nod to Peter Gordon, this is based on one of his recipes. I have made this so many times, it changes according to the fruit you use so can be different every time. Avoid blueberries as part of your fruit puree though, they don't do anything for this dish, but they work well on the side as an accompaniment with raspberries.

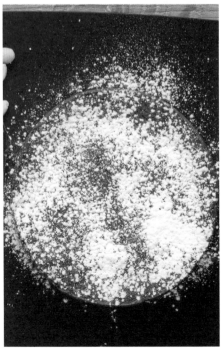

torta Barozzi with mascarpone cream

ingredients:

35g whole blanched almonds
35g whole peeled peanuts
50g unsalted butter
125g chocolate (at least 70% cocoa solids)
30ml strong espresso coffee
1 tbsp rum
2 large eggs, separated
110g caster sugar

for the mascarpone cream:
125g mascarpone
1 tbsp icing sugar
½ tsp vanilla bean paste
75ml double cream lightly whipped

method:

-preheat the oven to 180°C/350°F/Gas4
-place the almonds and peanuts on a baking sheet and roast for 4 minutes, set aside to cool, then grind in a small food processor to a coarse powder.
-reduce the oven temperature to 150°C/300°F/Gas2.
-grease and base line a 20cm springform tin.
-bring a saucepan of water to the boil and sit a large bowl on the top with the butter in to melt.
-when the butter has melted turn off the heat to the pan and add the chocolate, rum and coffee to the butter and allow to melt slowly with the bowl still sitting on the pan. Stir to create a smooth chocolatey mixture.
-when all the chocolate has melted remove the bowl from the pan and allow to cool a little.

-beat the egg yolks and sugar until thick and creamy, fold in the chocolate mixture and the ground nuts.
-in a clean glass bowl whisk the egg whites to soft peaks and then fold into the chocolate mixture.
-pour the cake mixture into prepared tin, and place in the preheated oven for 30-35 minutes, when cooked it should be a little sticky in the middle.
-take the cake out of the oven and leave to cool in the tin for 5 minutes.
-run a knife around the sides of the tin, release the outside of the tin and then turn the cake out onto a cooling rack and remove the baking paper. Allow to cool thoroughly.
-at this point the cake can be frozen for 2 months well wrapped.
-to make the mascarpone cream, mix together the mascarpone, sugar and vanilla until smooth.
-lightly fold in the whipped cream.
-refrigerate until required.
-place the torta Barozzi on a serving plate bottom side of the cake up and sift with icing sugar. Serve with a good dollop of the mascarpone cream.

serves 6-8.

Italy featuring again here, this is my version of the famous torta Barozzi from Modena. It has a secret ingredient (possibly balsamic vinegar) and I have chosen to use rum, but try it with balsamic. It is rich dark and positively cries out for the mascarpone cream to go with it!

meringue roulade with passionfruit, orange and raspberry cream

ingredients:

method:

4 egg whites
200g caster sugar
25g flaked almonds
330ml double cream
½ orange, zest and juice
2 passionfruit, halved and seeds removed
1 tbsp orange liqueur (Raisthrope orange/
Drambuie)
1 tbsp icing sugar
2 x 125g punnets raspberries

-preheat the oven to 200°C/375°F/Gas5.
-whisk the egg whites until stiff and dry, add the caster sugar a dessert spoon at a time, waiting until each spoonful has been well incorporated into the egg white. When all the sugar has been added it should be very thick, smooth and glossy.
-tear off a sheet of baking paper, big enough to line a swiss roll tin (see p. 131). Use a little of the meringue to dot in each corner and the middle of each side of the swiss roll tin. Then press the baking paper down and this will hold the paper down for you when you spread the meringue.

-spoon the meringue onto the paper and spread out evenly, taking care not to get too much up the sides of the paper as the meringue will tear when you come to remove the paper. Scatter the flaked almonds over the top of the meringue.
-place in the preheated oven, close the door and turn down the oven to 170°C/325°F/Gas3. Cook for 15 minutes until well risen and golden.
-take the meringue out of the oven and leave to cool in the tin.
-whisk up the cream with the sugar, orange juice, zest and liqueur until it just starts to form soft peaks, fold in the passionfruit seeds (the passionfuit will thicken the cream, so do not overwhip it).
-tear a piece of greaseproof paper large enough to tip the meringue out onto. Carefully turn the cooled meringue out and remove the bottom layer of baking paper. Spread with the cream and cover with the raspberries.
-starting with the shortest end nearest you roll up the roulade.
-wrap in the greaseproof, and keep in the fridge until ready to use.

serves 6-8.

I can't tell you how many times I have made this roulade, it's the showstopper dessert on the Gold Duke of Edinburgh residential cookery course, and never fails to delight as long as they follow oven temperature instructions.

pears poached in red wine

ingredients:

4 Williams pears, or other squat shaped pears
375ml fruity red wine
4 cardamom pods lightly crushed
1 star anise
1 cinnamon stick
4 cloves
185g caster sugar
185ml boiling water

method:

-peel the pears leaving the stalk intact, slice off the bottom of the pear so you have a solid base to stand it up on, carefully remove the core, with a corer if you have one cut out a cone shape working from the bottom of the pear.
-place the pears in a sealable container with the red wine and all of the spices. Leave overnight turning if you need to, to ensure the pears develop a rich red colour.
-dissolve the sugar in a pan with the boiling water. remove the pears from the spiced red wine and pour the all of the red wine, including the spices, in with the sugar syrup. Simmer for 5 minutes.
-place the pears in the poaching liquor and simmer gently for 5 minutes and then turn and poach for a further 5-10 minutes until they are cooked but not too soft. This will depend on the ripeness of the pears.
-remove the pears from the cooking liquor and set aside to cool. Boil the cooking liquor rapidly to reduce until it turns syrupy, taking care, there's lots of sugar and it could burn.
-strain over the pears.

serves 4.

These keep well for a week or so and pair beautifully with the torta Barozzi (p. 95) or with the pear and almond tart (p. 103) as pictured.

thai fruit salad

method:

10g mint, leaves finely chopped
50ml coconut cream
10g ginger, peeled and finely chopped
juice 1 lime
1 tbsp palm sugar
1 red apple, cored and sliced
¼ pineapple, peeled, cored and cut into chunks
½ pomelo (or 1 pink grapefruit), peeled, pith removed
and cut into segments
1 mango, stone removed, peeled and cut into chunks
1 star fruit, sliced

-mix together the mint, coconut cream, ginger, lime juice
and sugar.
-stir the prepared fruit in very gently to coat.
-leave to chill in the fridge for 1 hour before eating, stir
gently again before serving.

serves 3-4

Fruit salad jazzed up with ginger, lime and coconut cream, find any exotic fruit you can to make a
difference to your usual fruit salad

pear and almond tart

ingredients:

for the sweet shortcrust pastry:
225g plain flour
55g icing sugar
110g chilled butter cut into cubes
1 egg

for the filling:
165g butter, softened
165g caster sugar
3 eggs, beaten
165g ground almonds
1 tbsp semolina
4 pears
golden caster sugar for sprinkling

method:

-put the flour, icing sugar and butter in a food processor and blend until the mix resembles fine breadcumbs.
-add the egg with the mixer going and process until the dough comes together. Tip the dough onto a floured board and shape into a thin round circle.
-roll out to a circle big enough to fill a 28x4cm flan tin. Ease the pastry right into the corners of the base and up the sides, then neatly trim the pastry. Prick the base with a fork. Put in the fridge to rest whilst you make the filling.
-preheat the oven to 170°C/340°F/Gas3.
-beat the butter with a hand mixer until pale and soft, add the sugar and continue to beat until pale and fluffy.
-add the egg a little at a time, beating well after each addition.
-fold in the ground almonds.

-take the pastry filled flan case out of the fridge.
-spoon in the almond paste and spread out evenly. Sprinkle with the semolina.
-peel, core and quarter the pears or cut into fans as you see on the picture. Arrange around the almond paste and then sprinkle with the golden caster sugar.
-place in the preheated oven for 30 minutes and cook until firm and golden. If after that time the mixture is still runny, turn down the heat to 160°C and cook until firm.

serves 10.

One of my lovely clients Wendy Thompson gave this recipe to the green Macmillan cookery book many years ago. Wendy's recipe used fresh apricots, I have made it multiple times with plums, pears, prunes, peaches, apples and recently changed the ground almonds for ground pistachios and paired that with fresh figs from the garden.

This recipe feeds 10 people, obviously it can be made smaller but you will have pastry left over. If wrapped well, it will freeze for up to 2 months. The filling is easily reduced in quanitity.

This recipe comes from the wonderful Chrissoula at Vilea Village in Crete. It's a fantastic way to use up old filo pastry and you'll be surprised at how delicious it is!

portokalopita (orange and filo cake)

ingredients:

for the cake:
zest of half an orange
2 eggs
100ml olive oil
100g caster sugar
125ml total Greek yoghurt
1 tsp vanilla essence
2 tsp baking powder
1 x 250g packet filo pastry

for the syrup:
300ml water
200g caster sugar
1 cinnamon stick
zest of half an orange

method:

-preheat the oven to 180°C/350°F/Gas4
-place all the cake ingredients, except for the filo, in a bowl and beat together until well combined.
-take each sheet of filo pastry, one at a time, and rip to shreds. As you rip the pastry add it to the cake batter and mix until it is all incorporated.
-lightly oil and line the base of a 20cm cake tin with baking parchment, then pour in the cake mixture.
-place in the preheated oven and bake for 25 minutes until risen, golden and firm.
-whilst the cake is cooking, put all the syrup ingredients into a saucepan, bring to the boil and simmer for 5 minutes.
-when the cake comes out of the oven, strain the hot syrup slowly over the cake and allow the liquid to sink in. When cool, remove from the tin and serve with some more Greek yoghurt.

serves 6-8.

triple chocolate brownies with salted caramel ice cream and chocolate sauce

ingredients:

275g plain chocolate (at least 70% cocoa solids)
275g unsalted butter
85g milk chocolate, cut into large chunks
85g white chocolate, cut into large chunks
85g pecans, broken into pieces
175g plain flour
1 tsp baking powder
4 large eggs, lightly beaten
1 tsp vanilla essence
325g caster sugar

for the ice cream:
200ml caramelised condensed milk
300ml double cream
½ tsp sea salt flakes

for the chocolate sauce:
120g caster sugar
30g cocoa
a pinch of salt
60ml water
30g butter
½ tsp vanilla essence

method:

-preheat the oven to 170°C/325°F/Gas3. Line a 24cmx24cmx3.5cm tin with baking parchment (see p. 131).
-put the plain chocolate and butter in a large bowl, place over a pan of simmering water, turn off the heat and allow the chocolate to melt.
-sieve the flour and baking powder into a bowl.
-when the chocolate is melted remove from the heat.
-stir in the sugar, add the eggs and vanilla essence to the chocolate, then fold in the flour, nuts and remaining chocolate pieces.
-pour the chocolate mixture into the prepared tin. Place in the oven and bake for 20-25 minutes. The top should be firm but the inside should still feel soft, i.e. still have a slight wobble. It should still be gooey.
-allow the brownies to cool in the tin, when it is cool cut into squares. The size of the squares depends on your level of chocolate addiction!
-whip the caramelised condensed milk, cream and salt together until it is stiff.
-pour into a container.
-freeze overnight.
-to make the chocolate sauce mix together the caster sugar, cocoa, and salt together in a saucepan, mix in the water and then add the butter.

-place over a moderate heat and stir continuously until the butter has melted and the sauce comes to a gentle simmer.
-turn off the heat and add the vanilla essence.
-the sauce can be served warm or cold with the ice cream and brownies.

serves 8

Indulgence of the highest order, try warming the brownies for a finger licking dessert.

hazelnut and chocolate dacquoise

ingredients:

for the chocolate mousse:
2 sheets leaf gelatine
150g dark chocolate (at least 70% cocoa solids)
60ml milk
2 tbsp coffee liqueur
200ml cream, whipped to soft peaks

for the dacquiose:
85g blanched hazelnuts (see p. 131 for tips)
80g caster sugar
6 egg whites
75 g icing sugar plus extra, sifted, for dusting

method:

-to make the chocolate mousse: place the leaf gelatine in a shallow dish filled with cold water to soak .
-place the chocolate in a heatproof bowl.
-half fill a saucepan with water and bring to the boil, then turn off the heat.
-place the bowl containing the chocolate over the saucepan, taking care the water does not touch the bowl.
-stir occasionally until smooth.
-heat the milk until it just starts to steam, squeeze the water out of the leaf gelatine and whisk quickly into the milk, add the coffee liqueur and stir until smooth. Allow to cool a little before mixing slowly into the melted chocolate.

-set aside to cool, keeping an eye on it that it doesn't set. When cool to the touch fold in the cream and refrigerate until needed.
-pre heat the oven to 180°C/350°F/Gas4.
-grease and line the base and sides of two 24 cm x 30 cm baking tins.
-then make the dacquiose. Combine the hazelnuts and caster sugar in a small food processor and process until the hazelnuts are ground into a fine powder.
-beat the egg whites with an electric hand whisk until soft peaks form.
-slowly add the icing sugar a spoonful at a time beating well until the mixture is firm and glossy.
-gently fold ithe hazelnut mixture into the egg whites.
-spread evenly into the prepared tins to an even thickness.
-bake for 15 to 20 minutes or until golden and firm to the touch.
-cut out 24 rounds using a 4cm cutter while still warm.
-to assemble: spoon the mousse into a piping bag with a large star nozzle and pipe onto 8 of the dacquiose rounds.
-top each one with another dacquiose.
-pipe on another layer of mousse and put on another dacquiose.
-dust lightly with icing sugar.
-serve chilled. These can be kept in the freezer until required, taking out 30 minutes before you want to eat them.

serves 8 as a selection of desserts.

These little beauties take a bit of making but are ideal for a stress free dessert straight from the freezer, just remember to take them out 30 minutes before you need them.

sweet treats and bread

sticky toffee cupcakes

ingredients:

90g dates pitted and chopped
½ tsp bicarbonate of soda
110ml boiling water
40g very soft butter
75g dark soft brown or muscovado sugar
1 egg lightly beaten
½ tsp vanilla extract
90g self raising flour, sifted

for the caramel:
30ml boiling water
70g caster sugar
40 ml double cream
½ tsp vanilla extract
¼ tsp table salt

for the buttercream:
¼ tsp table salt
½ tsp vanilla extract
85g butter
85g icing sugar
2 dates for decoration

method:

-preheat the oven to 180°C/350°F/Gas4
-place the chopped dates in a small bowl with the bicarbonate of soda and boiling water and set aside for 20 minutes.
-prepare the salted caramel by pouring the boiling water over the sugar in a small saucepan and slowly heating to dissolve the sugar. Once the sugar has dissolved boil rapidly until the sugar syrup starts to caramelize.
-when the syrup starts to change colour, remove from the heat and carefully pour in the cream, salt and vanilla essence, it will splutter and spit a lot, but stir well to combine. Don't worry it will look strange at first but will come together to form a lovely rich fudgy caramel. Pour it into a bowl and allow to cool.
-beat the sugar and butter together for the cupcakes until light and creamy for about 5 minutes, either in a food mixer or in a bowl with an electric beater.
-add the egg slowly adding a tablespoon of the flour halfway through to stop the mixture from curdling.
-add the dates in their water and the vanilla extract, mix well then fold in the remaining flour.

-place 8 large bun cases in a muffin tray and divide the mixture between them (about a large tablespoon in each)
-place in the preheated oven for 20 minutes until risen and firm to the touch.
-leave for a couple of minutes and then remove from the muffin tray and place on a cooling rack.
-whilst the cupcakes are cooling prepare the icing. Beat the butter until very soft and add the icing sugar. Beat for a few minutes until it is very light and creamy. Add the cooled caramel, salt and vanilla and beat again until all is well combined together.
-when the cupcakes are cool, pipe or spread the icing over the cupcakes and decorate with a slice of pitted date.

makes 8.

Sticky toffee pudding in a bun- try doubling the recipe to make a 20cm sticky toffee sandwich cake.

orange and hazelnut biscuits

ingredients:

100g very soft unsalted butter
75g golden caster sugar
1 egg yolk
115g self raising flour
zest of ½ orange, finely grated
a few drops of sweet orange oil (available at Lakeland)
60g whole roasted hazelnuts roughly chopped (as per energy ball recipe p. 13)

method:

-cream the butter and sugar thoroughly until pale and fluffy.
-add the egg yolk, sifted flour, zest, oil and nuts and beat together with a wooden spoon or spatula.
-form the mixture into two balls and roll each one out onto a lightly floured surface in both hands until you have two sausage shapes about 5cm in diameter.
-lay a sheet of cling film on your work surface and wrap the biscuit mix up in the cling film, twisting the ends tight to make a neat sausage shape. Repeat with the other sausage of biscuit mix.

-refrigerate until chilled (overnight is best) or freeze until required (up to a month). Allow to soften a little from frozen before trying to slice.
-preheat the oven to 170°C/335°F/Gas3
-unwrap and slice into into 1cm rounds.
-place the dough slices onto a baking parchment lined baking tray (see p. 131) making sure they do not touch, and cook for about 8 minutes.
-they should not colour significantly and remember that a minute too far and they will burn.
-remove from the oven and immediately place onto a cooling tray with a palette knife taking care as they will be easily broken at this stage but will firm up very quickly.

makes about 36.

These biscuits are a good standby to have in your freezer, take out the sausage shaped raw dough, allow to defrost a little and then bake- try not to eat too many!

chocolate and sloe gin truffles

ingredients:

150g plain chocolate (at least 70% cocoa solids)
150ml double cream
25g unsalted butter
2 tbsp sloe gin

coating:
100g plain chocolate (at least 700% cocoa solids)
30g white chocolate

method:

-break the chocolate into squares and place in a bowl or food processor.
-grind the chocolate until it looks granular, like sugar.
-place the cream, butter and sloe gin into a small saucepan.
-bring to simmering point.
-with the motor switched on, pour the cream mixture into the processor and blend until it is smooth.

-pour the liquid into the 24 hole round chocolate mould sheet (see below), cool thoroughly.
-freeze overngiht.
-bring a pan of water to the boil, switch off and melt the dark and white chocolate, for the coating, in separate bowls over the just boiled water.
-push the frozen truffles out of the moulds and dip one at a time in the melted plain chocolate, then place on a tray lined with greaseproof paper. Drizzle the white chocolate over to decorate.

makes 24

I usually provide these after dinner at parties that I cater for, they are a two day job, and well worth sourcing the round silicone chocolate mould sheet from Lakeland (not the rectangular ones). They keep in a tin in the fridge for 2 weeks (if you're lucky!).

foccaccia with rosemary salt

ingredients:

method:

250g strong white plain flour
1 x 7g sachet easy blend yeast
1 tsp table salt
2 tbsp olive oil
200ml warm water
a little semolina flour (see p. 59)
½ tsp sea salt
1 tbsp chopped rosemary
extra virigin olive oil for drzzling

-place flour, yeast, salt, olive oil and 150ml of the warm water into a large bowl. Gently stir together with a wooden spoon to form a dough in the bowl gradually adding the remaining water to make a sticky dough.
-stretch the dough by hand in the bowl, pulling from the sides and then tucking into the centre turning 45 degrees each time. Repeat this process for 5 minutes. It will be very sticky.

-turn out the dough onto an oiled work surface and knead for 5 minutes more, it should still be quite sticky, but as you knead will firm up slightly. Try not to add too much extra flour .
-put back into an oiled bowl and cover with a teatowel. Leave in a warm place to rise for about 1 hour until doubled in size.
-sprinkle a tin with semolina flour. Tip your dough onto a lightly floured work surface and knock the dough back by kneading again for a couple of minutes. Press the dough out into the tin to about a 3 cm thickness. Leave to prove for 1 hour covered with a teatowel.
-preheat the oven to 220°C/425°F/Gas7.
-score the dough lightly with a diamond pattern using the tip of a sharp knife and make indentations all over with the tips of your fingers. Drizzle with some more olive oil, scatter over the sea salt and rosemary.
-bake in the preheated oven for 20-25 minutes until risen and golden. Drizzle with extra virgin oilive oil and serve warm.

makes 1 loaf.

After watching the bakers on the Great British Bake Off struggle with focaccia, I realised I wasn't making my dough wet enough, so here is a version of Paul Hollywood's technical challenge for you to try. Don't wear your best clothes whilst making this as it gets very messy and very sticky.

drinks

mint tea

ingredients:

3-4 stalks of fresh mint

method:

-pour boiling water over the mint, enough to make a couple of cups of tea.
-leave for 3-4 minutes to infuse and strain into teacups.

After an unfortunate bout of food poisoning in France my great friends James and Christine Marr took me to the amazing Colombe D'Or in St Paul de Vence, they had a delicious meal and all I could manage was a mint infusion, but it was perfect and I have been reproducing it ever since along with other flavours, and thankfully without food poisoning!

ginger and lemongrass tea

ingredients:

1 stalk of lemongrass, cut in half and bashed with a rolling pin
3 slices of fresh ginger, unpeeled

method:

-pour boiling over the lemongrass and ginger.
-leave to infuse for 3-4 minutes and strain into teacups.

cocoa chai

ingredients:

chai syrup:
1 litre water
4 yorkshire teabags
80g light soft brown sugar
40g fresh ginger, unpeeled and sliced
3 sticks of cinnamon
2 star anise
15 cloves
15 cardamom pods, lightly crushed

for drink:
4 tbsp chai syrup
2 tsp cocoa powder

200ml full fat milk

method:

-put all the ingredients into a saucepan, bring to the boil, reduce to a simmer and cook for 30 minutes.
-strain through a fine seive into a jug and keep in a jar or bottle.
-to make drink, mix together syrup and cocoa powder, whisk in milk, pour into a saucepan and whisk until it just comes to the boil.

I have included also a chocolate chai which I drank far too much of in Canada whilst producing the food for the photographs in this book, bear in mind a lot of the time it was -20 outside! I couldn't miss including elderflower cordial in this book, one year I made about 200 litres, many people have helped me make this, from Kiwi rugby players to Anthropology PHD students, but there's always a black Labrador or two with me when I go foraging for the flowers.

elderflower cordial

ingredients:

10 heads elderflower
1 lemon, zested and sliced
1 kg granulated sugar
900 ml water
45g citric acid

method:

-shake the elderflower heads to remove any unwanted visitors and place in a large sealable container with the lemon zest and slices.
-bring the water to the boil in a large saucepan, add the sugar and bring to the boil again to dissolve.
-pour the boiling syrup carefully over the flowers and lemons, add the citric acid and stir well.
-cover with a lid and leave for 24 hours.
-strain through a double layer of butter muslin in a sieve, or a jelly strainer.
-pour into sterilised bottles and keep in the fridge or freeze for up to 6 months in plastic bottles, makes about 1 ½ litres.

To sterilise glass bottles: run through a dishwasher then place in a cold oven making sure you have removed and plastic lids or tops. Bring the oven temperature to 140°C and then the bottles will be sterilised.

My star rating

Tiki, Marika and Hugo

Hugo

Hugo and Painslack sunrise

Christmas in the Dolomites

Posing for a treat

Pistachio and fig tart

Francesca and I.

Foraging for crab apples

Treat time again

Hugo in Slovenia

Mum at her first
grandchild's wedding

Very spoilt dogs

Antonio and drunk cheese!

Alison Sutcliffe's pork loin.

Autumn sunrise and cocoa chai

A summer meal

Elderflower foraging

More spoilt dogs.

Bruschetta

sunrise dogs

Painslack dogs with visiting
Duggle-dogs.

Summer dessert for a client

Yorkshire Pudding success 127
at the Yorkshire Wold
Cookery School

First school picture of me age 5

Grandpa Holtby and I

Mint jelly

Having fun making pasta

Canapé selection

Mass lasagne production

Mary Berry and I circa 1996

Injured hugo and stick!

Fresh figs from the garden

Injured hugo

Pimms jelly

Cooking in the
Dordogne, 1997

128

my favourite suppliers:

Dairy:
St Quintin's Creamery

Fruit and veg and local cheese:
Rafters of Driffield
shop.myvegbox.com

Fish:
H Peck and Son, Wednesday Market,
Beverley

Smoked salmon:
Staal's smokehouse
staalsmokehouse.co.uk

Meat:
Bluebell Farm (Alison Sutcliffe), Wetwang.
Burtons Butchers, Pocklington

Thai ingredients:
Thai food online
thai-food-online.co.uk

Equipment:
Lakeland Limited
www.lakeland.co.uk
Barnitts of York
barnitts.co.uk

Wine and Deli:
Roberts and Speight, Beverley
robertsandspeight.co.uk

Nuts, flours, sugars and dried goods:
Shepcote limited, Driffield
shepcote.co.uk
Whole Foods online
buywholefoodsonline.co.uk

Alphonso mango:
Makkah International Food, Hull Road, York.

Booker cash and carry/Amazon:
Callebaut 70% cocoa, milk and white
chocolate callets

Tesco:
Theo's Filo pastry

Balsamic vinegar:
Yorkshire drizzle
yorkshiredrizzle.co.uk

Stockists of Yorkshire ingredients:
William's Farm Kitchen at Tong Garden Centre
tonggardencentre.co.uk
The Farm Shop at Cranswick
farmshopatcranswick.co.uk

Yorkshire Rapeseed Oil
https://www.yorkshirerapeseedoil.co.uk/ (Rafters
of Driffield stock this)

Orange Liqueur:
Raisthorpe Manor
raisthorpemanor.com

Beer:
Wold Top Brewery
woldtopbrewery.co.uk

Wine:
Howard's Folly
howardsfollywine.com

Flours:
EB Bradshaw and Sons avilable at Bell Mills
Garden Centre, Driffield

behind the scenes in Canada

a few extra tips, tricks and suggestions:

-Always put a damp piece of kitchen roll or a damp flat sponge under your chopping board to hold it steady on your work surfaces.

-Always sharpen knives before you start chopping.

-Use digital scales to measure everything accurately, remember a litre of water weighs a kilo, its much easier to get the right liquid measurement on a scale than a jug.

-Use a teaspoon to scrape the skin off ginger, wastes a lot less than using a knife.

-With lemongrass stalks you need to remove most of the outer leaves of the lemongrass as they are inedible. You end up with a very small amount, which is much softer, in the centre of the lemongrass stalk. This is the only part that is edible. There is no need to waste the outer leaves as you can use them, along with ginger peelings, spring onion tops etc to make a nice fragrant stock for cooking rice.

-To peel garlic, place the garlic on a chopping board, large cooks knife laid flat on top and press down hard. This will lightly crush your garlic and make it easier to peel. Then sprinkle a little sea salt on top of the peeled garlic, crush into the board using the flat tip of your knife, crush the garlic into the board bringing the knife towards you. The salt acts as an abrasive.

-Let all citrus fruit come to room temperature before squeezing.

-Use full fat milk for cooking with. Only ever use double or whipping cream for boiling/making sauces, single will split. the same applies to crème fraiche and yoghurt.

-Bring meat to room temperature before cooking, about an hour in the kitchen, dependant on the size of the cut of meat.

-Never overcrowd a frying pan when browning meat, do it in batches a little at a time, or else it will most likely sweat and not brown.

-Oil a steak, or any other meat or fish for frying, rather than pouring oil into a frying fan, gives direct heat to the meat or fish and avoids smoking and fat spitting.

-Rest meat well after cooking. Steaks for about 10 minutes and a roast joint for up to an hour but at least 20 minutes. This gives you time to make a lovely gravy and will give you extra juices from the rested meat.

-I prefer to steam potatoes, rather than boil, especially for mashing and roasting as it stops them from absorbing too much water. For really crispy roast potatoes, steam potatoes until they start to soften on the outside, heat equal quantities of goose fat and rapseed oil in a roasting tin in a very hot oven for 5 minutes, shake the steamed potatoes well in the steamer and then very carefully tip into the very hot fat. To make them extra crispy on the outside, scrape each side of the pieces of potato with a fork, and then roast for 45 minutes at 180°C/350°F/Gas4. Take out of the oven, turn the potatoes, then put back in the oven for another 12-20 minutes until golden on all sides.

-For some of these recipes it is essential use silicone coated baking parchment not greaseproof baking parchment as it will stick. Baking parchment is available from the cash and carry or slighly more expensive, Lakeland.

-If you can only find hazelnuts with skins on, toast as per the recipe and when they are cool enough rub between your hands to remove the skin, return to the oven if they need browning a bit more, but beware they go from lovely light golden to black bullets in the wink of an eye, and taste horribly bitter.

-Try to cook with wine that you or others would happily drink.

-I always use large eggs, unsalted butter, sea salt and ground black pepper unless otherwise specified.

-Obviously not all ovens are the same so adjust the temperature to suit your oven.

-tsp=teaspoon, tbsp=tablespoon.

allergens

I have decided not to include allergen symbols in this book. At the Yorkshire Wolds Cookery School we highlight all our recipes to show which of the 14 notifiable allergens each recipe contains. As I am not in control of the ingredients you as the cook uses, I cannot be certain of what allergens your own ingredients may contain, apart from the obvious. We have found that pesto, for instance, should not contain any nuts other than pine nuts but some brands contain almonds or other nuts as a bulking agent. It is therefore necessary that you rigorously check ingredients as they may have hidden allergens that you would not expect them to contain.

conversion table

metric	imperial	spoon conversions
7g	¼ oz	½ tbsp
15g	½ oz	1 tbsp
20g	¾ oz	1 ½ tbsp
25g	1 oz	2 tbsp
50g	2 oz	4 tbsp
75g	3 oz	6 tbsp
100g	4 oz	8 tbsp
125g	5 oz	11 tbsp
150g	6 oz	12 tbsp
175g	7oz	14 tbsp
200g	8 oz	16 tbsp
225g	9 oz	18 tbsp
250g	10 oz	20 tbsp
275g	11 oz	21 tbsp
300g	12 oz	23 tbsp

useful gadgets and equipment:

Hand blender with a small processor
kenwood triblade hdp103wg
www.kenwoodworld.com/uk

Food processor
magimix compax 3200
www.johnlewis.com

Stand mixer
www.kitchenaid.co.uk

Hand mixer
dualit
www.dualit.com/products/hand-mixers

Knives
Chefs knives
www.procook.co.uk/product/procook-gourmet-x30-knife-set-2-piece-santoku-set
Filleting knife
www.procook.co.uk/product/procook-gourmet-x30-filleting-knife-20cm-8
Vegetable knife
www.barnitts.co.uk/products/details/6634.html
Zester
www.barnitts.co.uk/products/details/6634.html

Knife sharpener
amazon, henkels knife sharpener

Measuring spoons
barnitts
www.barnitts.co.uk/products/details/237518.html

Weighing scales
barnitts
www.barnitts.co.uk/products/details/193803.html

Pasta machine
barnitts
kitchen craft imperia double cutter pasta machine sp150
amazon
kitchen aid electric stand mixer attachment
kitchen aid 5ksmpra pasta sheet roller and cutter set

Dariole moulds
lakeland.co.uk

acknowledgements:

To customers past and present, for their custom and kind words.

To my fabulous assistant Lizzie Burdass (2.0) who worked tirelessly making this book look as good as it does. She is now promoted to 12.0.

To my friends and family, who have helped in testing these recipes, particularly the Duggleby's, who are always keen for a tasting night.

To all the staff that have worked with me over the years, particularly Sue, Elaine, Dee and Annie...they always manage to have a laugh, whilst providing great service.

And to, Kathryn, for always managing to have a party without being at the party.

To all the staff at the Yorkshire Wolds Cookery School, for their comradeship and encouragement to me to keep going and for ensuring (I hope) that my recipe writing improved over the years!

To my fantastic suppliers, who provide the superb ingredients that I really don't have to do much with.

To Jordan Walmsley, for the great photos. we had a hectic five days shooting the food in a small kitchen in Ottawa, a big learning curve for both of us.

To Antonio and Francesca, our great friends from the Hotel Hieracon on the Isola di San Pietro, Sardinia for introducing me to the wonders of Sardinian hospitality, food and wine.

To Eric and Evelyn, my in-laws in Canada, for their encouragement and enthusiasm for the food delivered to them.

To my sisters, both who love food as much as I do. Vicky for her introduction to all things Cretan and the best olive oil and oregano you have ever tasted, not to mention Yia Yia's stuffed courgette flowers. Anne, for keeping the family get togethers going after we lost Mum and the wonderful occasions with far too much great food and wine with our ever-growing family.

To my sons Tom and Charlie, for their input and encouragement and shared love of cookery programmes, new recipes and for finding great new places to eat.

Laura for her endless help at the sink and choice of photos and dishes. To all their friends who love to come and try out food at our house, who all share our love of food, crazy conversations, kitchen discos and parties.

Finally, to Robert who has given me the incentive and encouragement to write this book. Travelling has brought a new meaning to me, whacky races some might say - but it's never dull and the food we have found along the way has been amazing. Thankyou!

Index